Understanding Admissions:

Getting into the Top Graduate Schools in Computer Science and Engineering

Ramgopal Mettu   Ryan Lilien

www.UnderstandingAdmissions.org

Admissions@UnderstandingAdmissions.org

Contents

Chapter 1

Introduction

The main goal of this book is to eliminate the mystery surrounding the process of applying to a PhD program. Too frequently, students become intimidated by the process because it is unfamiliar. Most students don't have any real knowledge of the application process or what constitutes a strong doctoral candidate. This book will put you at ease and provide an insider's view of graduate admissions. If you follow our advice, we guarantee that you will improve your chances of being admitted to the research graduate program of your choice. The goal of any application is to make yourself as appealing as possible. To do this effectively, you need to know what the admissions committee is looking for. Through eleven chapters we will explain how to make your application as appealing as possible, describe how PhD programs evaluate and accept applicants, and provide criteria by which you can evaluate programs before and after you apply. By understanding the nuts and bolts of the application process, you will have the best chance to get into a program that will help you realize your career goals.

We also wanted to make this book broadly applicable and easy to use. So rather than being specific to a single discipline, we focus on the common criteria used to evaluate applicants in most doctoral programs in the sciences. This book will therefore be most useful for those interested in learning more about the application process to join a doctoral program in engineering, computer science, or natural sciences at a North American university. To make this book easy to use, we have structured the chapters to provide a step-by-step overview of gaining admission to graduate programs in the sciences. You will also be able to go back to selected chapters and read them in more detail during the process of applying to, and evaluating offers from, graduate programs of your choice. Although most readers will likely be undergraduate students, our advice is equally applicable to those who have worked in industry or are applying as they complete a Masters program.

Of course, there are plenty of sources of advice for getting into graduate school. What makes this book special is that you will get information and advice from faculty that have served on admissions committees and reviewed thousands of graduate school applications. The information contained in this short book is distilled from giving talks to, and running information sessions for, prospective students, as well as from giving advice to undergraduate advisees at our own institutions. Having participated in these activities, we know what works and what doesn't in a graduate school application, the hallmarks of a successful graduate program, as well the habits and practices you should adopt to

Prior to Application Year	Year of Application

• Engage Faculty and Letter Writers
• Explore Areas of Research Interest
• Participate in Summer Internship/
  Research Experience
• Compile Preliminary List of Programs
	• Letters of Reference (Aug/Sep)
	• Application Materials Available (Sep/Oct)
	• Application Materials Completed (Nov)
	• Letters of Reference Submitted (Oct/Nov)
	• Application Submitted (Dec)
	• Notifications of Acceptance (Mar/Apr)
	• Visit Programs as a Prospective Student
	  (Mar/Apr)

succeed after you get in. The decision to go to graduate school is a 4-6 year commitment, and we feel that everyone (including members of admissions committees that will read your application) is best served by your having a full understanding of what is involved in getting a Ph.D.

How This Book Is Organized

This book is organized in eleven chapters that each cover an important aspect of applying to, or succeeding in, a graduate program of your choice. We have tried to keep the discussion relatively informal. Reading this book from beginning to end before starting your application will give you an overview of how graduate programs in the sciences work. However, as you select schools and work on your application, you will also be able to consult specific chapters for advice. Chapter 2 focuses primarily on what graduate school is all about, and how it differs from what you have seen as an undergraduate. Chapter 3 will help you identify those around you that can give you one-on-one advice about being in graduate school. It is important to know what graduate programs in the sciences are looking for in their students, and how they evaluate applications; Chapters 4 and 5 cover this topic. Chapter 6 discusses the different aspects of a graduate program that determine its quality, both in its national ranking as well as in the ways that will help you achieve your career goals.

In, Chapter 7, we outline the elements of a graduate school application, and give a detailed description of how to tailor each part of the application to maximize your chances of admission to the program of your choice. Chapter 8 focuses on how to get a strong letter of reference in support of your application. Once you have gotten in to one or more programs, Chapter 9 provides a number of ways in which you can dig deeper to figure out which of your choices will best suit your career goals. If you haven't gotten into a program of your choice, we give some advice about how to follow up and improve a future application in Chapter 10. Finally, in Chapter 11 we give you a brief primer on how to approach your first year as a graduate student, and give some advice on the habits and practices that can help you be successful.

The Timeline

As with most applications, graduate schools have strict deadlines by which you must submit your materials. Generally speaking, these deadlines are in early December; you should give yourself plenty of time to prepare your application and to obtain the necessary letters of reference. In fact, you would ideally begin thinking about your application, and evaluating programs in the summer before the admission deadline. Prior to that, you should take opportunities to engage faculty and explore areas of interest. Near the end of the summer of your third year, you should identify and approach faculty to ask for letters of recommendation. By doing this early, you give them plenty of time to write a strong letter. Then, you have the Fall semester to put together and submit your materials. Admissions committees will generally take 3-4 months to review applications, and you will receive notifications from programs in early to mid-Spring. The figure above summarizes this timeline by outlining the important events in the application and admission process.

We have written this book to be concise enough to be useful, but detailed enough to include those aspects of graduate applications that we have found are routinely overlooked. Spending a few hours reading these pages will help you not only in putting together a polished (and successful) application and a "bigger picture" of the journey that you are beginning. It is our hope that by giving simple and effective strategies for each part of the application process, we are helping you to begin a rewarding journey to obtaining your doctorate.

Chapter 2

Deciding to Attend Graduate School

So you've decided to attend graduate school. While there are a number of good reasons to apply to graduate school, there are also a number of bad reasons. In our experience, students who have thought through the process and have applied for good reasons generally are more successful than those who have not. Graduate school is more than simply "something to do." It's something that one should be passionate about. Of course you're not going to be excited about every aspect of graduate school - no one is excited about every aspect of any career choice. But you should be excited about the majority of what takes place. The goal of this chapter is to ensure that you're applying for the right reasons.

The first thing to think about is the "long-term" view. So we're not talking about 50 years from now; we're thinking about when you finish. What is the point of graduate school? It's not simply to waste time nor should it be thought of as a "job in science". A good graduate program should help you develop a number of skills. These are the skills that make a successful researcher. There are two primary categories of things you will learn in graduate school, the textbook knowledge of your specific field and how to think like a researcher. When you finish, you will likely be the world's expert in the somewhat narrow scientific discipline of your thesis project. Interestingly, this is a field that you may or may not pursue after graduation. As a Computer Science example, say your thesis is on non-linear dimensionality reduction for themed but unstructured experimental data. You are not likely to carry that specific project through to your retirement. It is possible that you will initially specialize in dimensionality reduction but most likely your specific research area will change through your career. You are of course not going to return to graduate school every time your research focus changes. This is why mastering the specifics of your thesis project is far less important than acquiring the skill of thinking like a researcher. The most important skills you will learn in graduate school are how to think analytically, how to ask the right questions, and how to solve research problems. Given this skill set you will be well equipped to tackle research in almost any problem domain. Of course this isn't strictly true - if you trained in computer science theory you can't claim to be an expert in theoretical physics; however, if you put in the effort you should be able to tackle a wide range of research problems within your discipline.

Here are a few things that you should learn in a good graduate program. These are also briefly described in Chapter 11 "Starting Out", but we introduce them here because they're important enough to list twice. If you are not interested in learning these skills then perhaps graduate school isn't for you. Of course a good graduate program should teach you how to conduct research, but what does that entail? It's primarily about developing the thought processes for analyzing research problems. You should learn to split a problem into parts and then to address each part. You should learn how to form a good abstraction for any research problem or process. You should learn how to identify 'good' research problems and more importantly how to identify 'bad' problems. You should learn the difficult to master skill of writing a scientific research paper. You should gain some experience writing a grant proposal. You should learn how to give a good, engaging, and informative research talk. You should gain the ability to critically read a research paper and to identify its strengths and weaknesses. You should gain the ability to teach or explain complicated topics to others. It's been said that you don't really understanding something until you can explain it to a ten year old.

Good and Bad Reasons to Attend Graduate School

Ok, so what are some good reasons to go to graduate school? First you should fundamentally be interested in the discipline and possibly a specific research problem. If you are truly interested in the material then going to graduate school will be fun. And that's important. If you don't enjoy the specifics, you are not likely to be fully engaged and are less likely to get the same benefit from being in the program. If you are interested, then you will, on your own, decide to follow interesting leads, go above and beyond what is required, and have an enthusiastic attitude. We will talk later about why these are important characteristics to have. Another great reason to attend graduate school is that you want a career in either academic or industrial research. Either way, if you want to lead a research group, if you want to guide research decisions then you need a Ph.D.

What are some bad reasons to go to graduate school? Going to graduate school because there's nothing else to do or because you don't yet know what you want to do are both bad ideas. If these are your reasons for applying you will not have sufficient motivation to succeed. If you get into a top program, the other students will run laps around you and you will not stand out. You may find that after a few years you will not have enough energy left to finish. Then you'll be faced with either leaving without a degree or muddling through for a few more years and then maybe leaving without a degree. Similarly, it is not good to apply because all your friends are applying. Nor is it a good idea to apply because you did not get an industry job.

There is one final bad reason for applying to graduate school that is a bit more subtle; because it doesn't sound so bad. Some people go to graduate school because they enjoyed undergraduate classes and they want to do that for a few more years. This may be a reason to do a course-only terminal masters degree; but, it is not a good reason to pursue a Ph.D. for the simple reason that courses are a small part of graduate school and an even smaller part of success in graduate school.

Neat Things about Being a Graduate Student

Being a graduate student is not always the grueling boot-camp that we make it out to be. There are a few really cool things about being a graduate student. First, in most programs you get paid in some form or another. Typically this comes in the form of a small stipend that is sufficient to cover living expenses. At some schools you can supplement your stipend by receiving external fellowships (from the government, non-profit institutions, or corporations) sometimes these are called "top-up awards".

Another benefit of graduate school is that you will be surrounded by a bunch of very smart people. The faculty, graduate students, and department visitors will provide lots of intellectual stimulation. They will serve as sounding boards for your research ideas and problems and you should take the time to learn what they are working on. Take advantage of this opportunity; nearly every researcher we know remembers graduate school as one of their most intellectually rich experiences.

As a graduate student, you will become an expert in your area of research. In fact, when you finish your Ph.D. you are likely the world's leading expert in your specific research area. It's very cool to be a thought leader working at the bleeding-edge of research and discovery. If you're in a good lab, your advisor and fellow lab mates will value your ideas and contributions. Of course you won't have this level of expertise in your first few years, but when you get there the journey will have been worth the reward. The notion of becoming a world expert raises another important point, that of balancing this specific expertise with broad knowledge. We will revisit this later.

Throughout graduate school you will have access to research ideas well before they hit the market. We can't tell you how many times we've seen a press release or popular news story about an exciting new technology that we can honestly say we knew about years before. Not only did we know about it years before, but in many cases we also know the researchers who developed it. We shouldn't have to convince you that it's cool to be one of the first people to play with new technology; but early access has other important advantages. If you stay abreast of what's happening in your field, you may be able to incorporate this inside information into your work before these advances are widely known.

As a graduate student you will have a fair amount of control over your daily schedule. There will certainly be meetings, courses, seminars, etc. But around these commitments you can structure your time in a way that makes most sense to you. For many graduate students this means working late into the night but not having to wake up super-early the next day. This is both good and bad. On one hand it allows you to structure your time in a way that makes you most efficient and it allows you to more easily schedule things like haircuts and dentist appointments. On the other hand it sets a bad expectation for the way things will be when you get your first job after graduation. Most likely your new employer, whether it is a university or a private company, will not be so flexible. It's also bad because it means that you have to be very diligent with respect to getting things done. We've seen countless cases where graduate students simply don't get enough done each week. Learning to work efficiently and effectively is another skill we would definitely add to our list of "what you'll learn in graduate school".

Perhaps an initially overlooked perk of graduate school is the opportunity to travel with all (or most) expenses paid to research conferences all over the world. Typically if you have a paper accepted to a conference and you have been invited to give an oral presentation, then there should be money to support your travel. These funds can come from your lab, your department, or an external fellowship provided by the conference itself. Attending conferences is a great deal of fun, but it's also a lot of work. Everyone has a different thought on how to approach research conferences. To us, research conferences are an amazing venue for idea generation and learning. We feel there are three primary activities you should be involved with at a conference, 1) attend most talks (but not necessarily all, be sure to leave time activities 2 and 3), 2) network with other researchers (meet new colleagues and reconnect with old ones), and 3) spend some quiet time thinking and developing your ideas. Interestingly, we often combine tasks 1 and 3; we find research talks an exceptionally rich and stimulating environment in which to develop new ideas. You will get a lot out of attending research conferences and it is a really neat aspect of being an academic.

Graduate School versus Undergraduate Education

We've discussed a number of reasons to attend, but we haven't focused on the significant differences between graduate training and undergraduate education. Rather than pure classroom-based learning, you will spend most of your time in the research lab, learning to think, to ask 'the right' questions, and to solve problems. Even in your coursework you will likely discuss research topics/ideas that are new and not completely fleshed out. In undergraduate education, students who excel in structured, textbook-guided, lecture-based courses and who are good test takers can obtain top grades (A or the equivalent). This is not always the case in graduate school. When working on a problem as an undergraduate, you knew the problem had a solution and you knew approximately how long it should take to solve (*i.e.*, it should be possible to complete a weekly problem set in one week using available resources). As a graduate student, the solvability of the problems you tackle is unknown and it is unclear what resources you will need to solve your problem. Of course, if you are in a good lab, most likely your advisor will know the feasibility of your research project (that is why they are the advisor) but they could be wrong. In other words, in graduate school you don't know if your research project can be completed in 1 month, 6 months, 12 months, or not at all.

As a graduate student in a North American university there are three types of courses you may take: undergraduate courses, lecture-based courses, and seminar-based courses. First, depending on your background, you may be required to take one or two undergraduate courses to fill any gaps in your existing knowledge. This is an opportunity for you to take these courses with a different eye. You may meet some advanced undergrads who are interested in your research and who may look to you for advice on graduate school. This is a neat experience. In addition, regardless of their research area, you should get to know the course instructor and any graduate student teaching assistants. Being known as an interested and friendly person around the department is always a good thing. Second, you will take traditional lecture-style courses. These are likely similar to those you completed as an undergraduate. The professor lectures during each class, there are assignments, and typically, exams or a final project. These are great opportunities for you to gain experience working on small, time constrained research-like projects. Finally, you will take seminar-based courses. In most seminar courses, the professor lectures during the first few meetings of the semester and then the course is handed over to the students. In subsequent weeks, students take turns presenting either seminal or cutting-edge papers preselected from the primary research literature. Seminar courses play several important roles in graduate education. Use them to improve your ability to efficiently read and evaluate papers, to gain experience participating in academic discussions, and to develop the skills and confidence to deliver high-quality research presentations. We will discuss seminar courses again in the last chapter.

Across all three types of courses, you'll be amazed at how your perspective has changed from the not-so-distant past when you were an undergraduate. For most undergraduates, courses fulfill requirements. As a graduate student you are like a hungry wolf looking for food. When you take a course as a graduate student, you should be thinking about how anything you learn could be used to advance your research project. In many cases, you will take a course explicitly because you need it for some aspect of your project.

Unlike the undergraduate experience, success is not strictly quantified by the grades you achieve. In graduate school, success relates more to research productivity. Measures of productivity, as imperfect as they may be, include the number of papers published and the number of conference presentations delivered. Strong graduate students have or develop excellent problem solving skills and can stay focused for extended periods of time. The most successful graduate students do not face fewer obstacles, rather they tend to not be derailed by the numerous setbacks of research. If you give up easily then graduate school is not for you. As a graduate student, you will learn that most research problems do not have a straightforward solution, and that most of the solutions you come up with don't work for most of the time you are working on them. Why? Simply put, that's research! If your research topic were easy, someone else would have done it already. If we know something to be true or that something will work in a certain way, then simply observing the phenomenon is not research. Here's an example we like to use. Consider being tasked with the project of building a chair. We know the resources and supplies necessary to build a chair and it is easy for us to estimate the time required for construction. Building a chair is not research. On the other hand, it's not immediately obvious that one could devise a general purpose time machine. Hopefully your research lies somewhat short of building a time machine, but you get the idea. Because research takes significant time to complete, you must be well motivated. Self-motivated. In fact, all permanent motivation is self-motivation. Someone (*i.e.,* your lab mates, advisor, friends, or family) can get you excited for a short time, but if the motivation does not come from an internal source it will fade. You must find the fire in your belly.

So You've Decided

Great! You've decided to start on an adventure that will span the next four-plus years of your life and your professional career. It's a rewarding experience. In the next chapter we will discuss obtaining advice and opinions from those around you. By collecting this information you will get a better picture of what graduate school is like, where to apply, and how to assemble your strongest application.

Chapter 3

Seeking Advice

Before you work on your application, it is very important to get a realistic picture of what graduate school is about, from a number of perspectives. You may not realize it, but these perspectives are all around you: the graduate students and faculty in your own department can be valuable sources of information that can help you decide how to select a graduate school as well as one or two research areas to pursue. In this chapter we will focus on the people around you that can provide valuable information about particular institutions, as well as general information about the pros and cons of graduate school life and the experience of getting a doctorate. We suggest that you read this chapter both now and after you have read the sections on applying to graduate school and evaluating your options once you've gained acceptance. On the first pass, you will get an idea of where the folks around you fit into the graduate school experience, and on the final pass you will be able to identify how to direct specific questions that you may have. If you go down the academic route, you'll undoubtedly be seeking advice regularly from peers and mentors; this is an essential part of academic interaction. Don't be intimidated, faculty are typically very welcoming to students interested in learning about advanced degrees.

It is important to note though, that although we will focus primarily on sources of advice in the university setting, it is certainly not the only place that you will find information. Indeed, you should not hesitate to get opinions from friends, family, or recent graduates. For graduate work in the sciences, keep in mind that speaking to people with research-oriented degrees, usually a Ph.D., rather than professional degrees, such as an M.D. or J.D., will yield the most relevant advice.

Perhaps the first and most direct source of information about graduate school are the faculty in your department. Faculty have built a career on academic teaching and research. They too were undergraduates who followed the path to graduate school, and then to a position in which they could mentor students. Moreover, it may even be the case that faculty in your department have attended the very schools you are considering. It is most useful to seek out faculty with whom you have had previous interaction (*e.g.,* an instructor in a course you particularly enjoyed), or a faculty member whose research area interests you. Speaking for ourselves and former colleagues, advising a bright and enthusiastic undergraduate about graduate school is a truly rewarding experience. Not only do we have a sense of nostalgia about our own experience and what we wished we had known, but we also get the opportunity to encourage a new member into the academic research community.

That said, faculty members are a busy bunch, and there are a few strategies that can maximize your chances of getting some face time. If you are an undergraduate at a research university, realize that faculty members are often inundated with email requests, so don't expect a prompt reply to your questions, or even to your request for an appointment. The best way to approach a faculty member is to visit them during office hours, a time during which faculty are somewhat free. Don't worry if you are not enrolled in a class with a particular faculty member; office hours are a regular time in which faculty must be available and they generally won't mind if you stop by. If you are an undergraduate at a college, or institution with modestly-sized graduate programs, then the task of getting advice from faculty should be relatively easy. In fact, you may have an assigned advisor or mentor who can direct you to faculty that may have connections to the very institutions you are interested in. Whether you are at a college or research university, the alumni network is an excellent resource to take advantage of. Generally, the undergraduate program director or department head keep close track of successful alumni (*e.g.*, those that have gone on to graduate school), and can likely give you a few contacts to get started.

Just as you have favorite topics in your degree program, graduate students in your department have pursued an advanced degree because of their specific interests. So, a good place to start is to simply approach the teaching assistants in your favorite classes. Ask them about their background, what schools they applied to and why they chose to attend your institution over another. Also, be sure to find graduate students at different phases in their degree; a first- or second-year graduate student can give you valuable information about how their undergraduate institution prepared them for graduate school, while third- or fourth-year students can generally give a better perspective on conducting scientific research, and what to look for in a research lab.

Last but not least, it is always a good idea to consult your institution's career center. While they will not have access to the focused perspective of people from your own department, a career center will be generally have access to a more well-developed alumni network of graduates from a number of different disciplines who are more likely to "cover" the set of schools you are interested in applying to. These alumni can likely give you general advice on the graduate student community at the institutions you will be applying to. Additionally, a career center can give you valuable critiques on both your resume and personal statement, both of which are important components of your application.

As you go through the process of seeking advice, it is important to be aware that each person you speak to will have their own particular view of applying to, and succeeding in, graduate school. Remember to take external advice seriously, but also with a grain of salt, since you must decide what is best for you and your goals. Finally, it is good practice in academia, and in life, to send a short email thanking those who have given you advice.

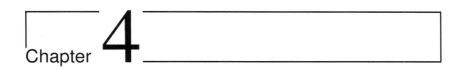

Chapter 4

What Schools are Looking For

If our assumption is correct, and you are looking to attend a North American research-oriented university, then the schools you will apply to are looking for one thing over everything else. In fact, your entire application is evaluated to assess you on this one particular skill. No, it's not your ability to get good grades, nor is it your ability to assume the presidency of thirty different undergraduate clubs and organizations. It's your ability to successfully contribute to a research program. Why? Faculty at top research schools are interested in research. Not incremental, turn-the-crank, get some output type of research, but cutting-edge, never-been-done-before, we-don't-know-if-it's-even-possible research. To accomplish this, faculty lead research groups of post-docs, graduate students, and undergraduate students (more on this organization later). The success of a research group is a function of its members. Faculty have to be convinced that if you join their group, that you will be a productive member of the team - that the team will be better with you on it.

We don't mean to paint faculty as evil overlords who organize their trainees to do their bidding. We're sure some faculty organize their labs that way and you should avoid these labs (see the section in the last chapter for tips on selecting a good lab group). Most faculty are genuinely excited about the educational process and they very much enjoy helping new students grow both as researchers and as individuals. But generally speaking, faculty fall along a spectrum. Faculty at smaller, less research-oriented schools tend to be more into the educational process than research while faculty at large research universities tend to be more intensely focused on research than teaching. Again, we don't want this to sound too harsh. This doesn't mean that they don't care about you or that they aren't going to help you. It simply means that faculty are excited about research and need to have strong research teams to help them accomplish their goals. They want to work with smart people and solve difficult problems. So, they are going to evaluate you on your current and potential ability to contribute to their research team.

So, given that there is no widely accepted "research aptitude test", how do they assess this ability? Faculty look for the following general skills.

- The ability to think analytically and solve complex problems.

- The ability to thrive in a competitive and fast paced environment.

- The ability to work quickly and to maintain a friendly go get'em attitude.

- The ability to work both independently and with others.

- The ability to be a project leader.

- The ability to function in English. If English is not your first language, you need to demonstrate that you can work in an English speaking lab. You will not be successful if a language barrier prevents you from interacting with your colleagues, giving presentations, writing papers, attending seminars, and so on. We've seen the language barrier pose a problem for many students. Don't simply assume that because you're a whiz in the technical material that that will make up for a lack of English skills.

- The ability to express your ideas coherently, through writing or presentation. This skill applies to both native and non-native English speakers and is different from the ability to function in English. We've known plenty of native English speakers who could not communicate their ideas. If you spend half the meeting with your advisor just trying to communicate you will be at a disadvantage.

- A lack of arrogance. The best way you can convince people that you are smart is simply to do great work and to help them do great work.

Each of the above skills are assessed by looking at your transcript, your undergraduate research and extracurricular record, your letters of recommendation, your personal statement, and phone interviews. This may seem like a lot, but we have a colleague who boils these skills down into three key factors. He looks for students who 1) are friendly and fun to work with, 2) are 'smart enough', and 3) walk quickly. Being friendly is obviously useful, but other two deserve additional explanation. What does it mean to be 'smart enough'. There's no single answer, but it means that you don't have to be the smartest person on the planet. You do have to be smart enough to fully understand the research problem and to make intellectual contributions. The threshold for this varies by field, department, and faculty. Ok, what's this about walking quickly? It was his observation (and we agree) that people who walk fast walk with a purpose and tend to be internally motivated. They walk fast because they are excited about getting where they are heading. This doesn't mean that slow walkers are not motivated; however, our empirical observations tend to support the connection between fast walkers and motivated people.

How do you convince the admission committee that you will be successful in a research program, given that you can't show them how fast you walk? The best evidence is of course that you've already done it. That you've been successful in a research environment. This means you should get involved in research as an undergraduate and you should get a strong letter of recommendation from the faculty supervising your research (see Chapter 8).

Undergraduate Research: The Most Important Thing You Can do for Your Application

What type of research should you get involved with? If possible, get involved in a project where you function as more than simply an extra set of hands. What looks better: A student who joined a large lab and who helped run errands for graduate students and postdocs or a student who joined a smaller lab, had his/her own small research project, and presented the result at their local undergraduate research showcase? The second student looks better because they have experience conducting research. The first student was simply in the vicinity of research and while this student may have learned a lot, there's a difference between passively learning and actively getting things done. If the second student does a good job they will be able to get a strong letter of recommendation from his/her advisor. This letter will describe the student as having the types of skills the admissions committee is looking for and it will provide situational examples where the student demonstrated those skills. If you're lucky the letter will describe your performance as similar to that of a first or second year graduate student. This clearly tells the admissions committee that you are ready.

You should look for a research experience where you can make an intellectual contribution. Finding an opportunity like this can be difficult, especially on the first try. You may need to take a more passive research role for a semester or two before you are assigned a research project of your own. During this time, you should be extremely ambitious. You should read all assigned papers (and probably more), you should spend more time in the lab than required, and you should engage in intellectual discussions with the graduate students in the group. Be careful not to go over the top. Look for subtle cues to determine if you're getting in the way. Grad students and faculty are busy and although they enjoy interacting with you, they do need time to complete their own work.

Once you've proven yourself you can ask to work on a project of your own. It's great if you can come up with an idea on your own. Because this is a difficult skill to learn and because your advisor likely has their own research agenda, it's likely that your advisor will modify your idea or push you towards something different. That's ok. Your advisor has significantly more research experience than you and will use this experience to guide you away from projects that are likely to fail. In many cases, your advisor will already know how to complete your entire project. They can see that a solution exists and that you should be successful. A good advisor will guide you towards the solution. Note that this is true of almost all undergraduate research and of most graduate research.

You should look for a lab where the students are happy and the faculty advisor has worked with undergraduates before. This is important because undergraduates are different than graduate students and your advisor needs to take that into consideration. This will play into the tasks and responsibilities assigned to you. By working with a professor that regularly supervises undergraduates you will improve your chances of research success. It's worth noting that undergraduate research experience can be setup as purely volunteer, for course credit, or for a small stipend. All of these arrangements are equivalent from the admissions committee's perspective.

Ok, so you're going to get involved in an undergraduate research project where you will actually be doing work. What else? Ideally the project should be in the same research area in which you are applying. Broadly speaking that means if you are a Computer Science major your research should be in Computer Science, but more specifically, if you are interested in graduate work in Machine Vision, then it would be good to find a project in Machine Vision or at least somewhere in Artificial Intelligence. Again, this speaks to your ability to be successful in the target graduate program. If you can't find a research project in your specific area (*i.e.,* Machine Vision) that's ok; however, for your research experience to appropriately influence the admissions committee it should be in the right department and as relevant as possible.

Consider the school you currently attend. It's reasonable to believe that a large research university with a well respected graduate program is the ideal place to get undergraduate research experience. However, a very research-oriented school can actually work against you. At large research-oriented universities, faculty have their pick of strong graduate students and postdocs. At these institutions, faculty often consider working with untrained undergraduates as something that detracts from their research. It consumes both the faculty's time and the time of students in the lab. A small college is not ideal either. The difficulty with a small college is that many faculty are focused on teaching and they don't conduct much research of their own. At a small school it can be hard to find opportunities in your research area. So if both big and small schools are not ideal, what should you do? Do the best you can. Be a problem solver. If there aren't many research opportunities at your school you just have to look longer, ask more times, and start earlier. If large research groups are hesitant to accept undergrads, you may have to start as a passive lab member, simply attending lab meetings and chatting (just a bit) with the graduate students. Show the lab that you are seriously interested and that you are not simply a student trying to add another activity to your resume.

We've glossed over the topic of where to find research opportunities. The best way is to ask faculty you know, professors from whom you've taken courses, or graduate students (perhaps your teaching assistants). Tell them that you are interested in eventually applying to graduate school and that you'd like to find a research opportunity in field X where you could both gain research experience and help the lab. If you get a no, ask if they could point you towards another group that may have an opening. Some departments advertise undergraduate research positions in a newsletter, email, or website. Ask your undergraduate student office.

If you are still unable to find a research opportunity, then the next best thing is to get involved with "project-based" extracurricular activities. For example, an inter-university robot competition, an electric car team, a green energy club, or a synthetic biology group. Look for a project where you can do research-like things as well as gain experience working with a group towards a common goal. If there is a faculty mentor, try to treat them as a research supervisor. This is most likely a person from whom you will get a letter of recommendation. In fact, perhaps the faculty mentor has a research group of their own and if you do an amazing job on the extracurricular project team, he or she may ask you to join their group (or you can ask them directly).

Some schools offer students the opportunity to complete an 'honors thesis' or 'senior thesis'. The scale and scope of these projects vary from school to school. Of course, if this is purely a senior thesis then it will occur too late in the application cycle to be of use for an application submitted that same academic year. Admissions committees evaluate these theses on a case by case basis. They will determine how much research experience the thesis provided. Completing a thesis will certainly not hurt your application, but it's not always a direct substitute for traditional research experience.

Another good possibility for gaining research experience is a summer position at a university other than your own. Unfortunately, these positions can be difficult to obtain. If you "cold email" faculty about research positions you are not likely to get a reply. This is not necessarily because you don't have the appropriate qualifications; but rather is because faculty get tons of emails from students throughout the year and many have adopted a policy of not replying to (or even reading) all messages. The best way to get "in" is to get an introduction from one of your current professors. Faculty are much more likely to reply to an email from another faculty, especially if it's someone they know. Ideally you would ask a professor from whom you've taken a class and received a top grade (*i.e.*, your course grade should be within the top 5-10% of the class). Tell the professor that you are interested in attending graduate school and are looking for interesting summer research opportunities in (your favorite research area) either at your or a different university. Mention that you are looking for an opportunity that would be mutually beneficial (*i.e.*, you want both to gain research experience and to help the lab). Spending time at a different university, particularly one where you may apply for graduate school has additional advantages. First, it's a great way to see if you like the school, department, and city. Second, it allows you to reach out and get to know some of the faculty. Letters of recommendation from professors at the university to which you are applying tend to be very influential. This works both ways, a good letter will really help your case, but a bad letter will almost certainly undermine your chances of getting in. Beyond getting a letter from a particular faculty, you may also decide which faculty you want to work with and possibly identify a potential research project.

Occasionally a summer research opportunity will come with a very modest stipend. If this happens, great; but if possible don't let the lack of a stipend push you away from an otherwise great opportunity. We realize this is easier said than done. Education is expensive and you do have to live somewhere and eat something. It may be possible to apply for external fellowships to support your summer research position. Ask your department's career office about possible opportunities. These can come from government, university, or private sources. If you qualify, the National Science Foundation (NSF) and National Institutes of Health (NIH) may have fellowships (*e.g.*, NSF Research Experience for Undergraduates (REU)). Applying to these programs typically requires a statement of interest and letters of reference, some of the same elements as your graduate school application. Thus you will need to focus on finding these opportunities relatively early.

Finally, if none of the above work for you, summer internships in industry can be a reasonable substitute experience. Be sure that the industry opportunity has a research or project based feel. If in doubt ask one of your faculty to help you evaluate the opportunity.

Other Activities and Over-Commitment

It's good to be involved in a few extracurricular activities. Involvement in these activities demonstrates that you can function outside the classroom. Although it's good to be involved in the right activities, it's not good to be involved in so many that your contribution to each is essentially zero. In other words, be aware of being over-committed. You want to have two things that you can write/speak about with competence and experience – this will be a very important element of your research statement. We would much rather work with a student who made major contributions to two projects than one who made minor contributions to a dozen projects. For at least one activity, try to assume a role more substantial than "member" (*i.e.*, try to take on a leadership role). Finally, while these activities improve your resume, keep in mind that non-academic letters of recommendation are worth significantly less than academic letters (see Chapter 8 for information on obtaining letters of recommendation).

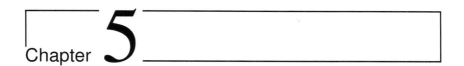

Chapter 5

How the Admissions Committee Reviews Your Application

So we've given you the main list of things we're looking for in a new graduate student. And you now have a plan of attack for acquiring these experiences and skills. Before we go into detail about how to prepare each of the components of your application, we think it's important for you to get a general idea of how your application is actually reviewed. After you finalize and submit your application materials, your application will eventually arrive at the target department. After your application is checked for completeness, it is forwarded to the admissions committee for evaluation. Admissions committees primarily consist of faculty and may also have one or two current graduate students. The committees follow different procedures at each institution, but their end goal is always the same: to admit an appropriate number of graduate students that best fit the needs of the department.

In nearly every admissions committee, applications will progress through several 'filters'. The first step is to filter applications using easy-to-evaluate criteria (such as GPA, test scores, rank of undergraduate institution). The goal is to perform a rapid first-pass through the applications to quickly identify and eliminate those applications that are clearly below the bar for that school. Some schools will aim to eliminate only 10% of the applications at this stage while others remove 30% or 50%. The value depends upon the number of applications received, the size of the admissions committee, and the selectivity of the program. Clearly, more people are below the bar at a stronger school than at a weaker one.

After applications have been filtered, committees will carefully review, rank, discuss, and decide which of the remaining students to admit. There are two general approaches to how this is done and most schools use a hybrid approach somewhere in between. The first category of admission is often referred to as the "best-athlete" model, and is somewhat common among the most competitive programs. Rather than performing a one-to-one assignment of students to faculty, best-athlete programs simply admit the students who have the strongest overall applications regardless of their stated interests. That is, students are accepted to the program, and initially funded, by the department, rather than by a single faculty member. In many top-ranked programs with large departments, it is the expectation that these students will find a research group matching their interests and become successful.

The second category of admission, which we like to call the "one-to-one" model, requires the admissions committee to filter applications based on a broad evaluation of GPA and test scores, and leaves detailed evaluations to individual faculty members who may "hire" you into their research group. In this model, individual faculty members who have openings in their research groups evaluate applications, searching for the best fit. Often, these faculty will contact students directly to try and assess whether a student has the chance to be successful in their group.

Regardless of the approach taken by the committee, several faculty members will carefully review your application. To give you an idea of what this entails, when we are asked to review an application, we do the following. First, we quickly check the university you attended and look at your overall grade average. Then we look at your resume or curriculum vitae (CV) for research activities. If you are applying from a weak school with weak grades and no research experience, then we've likely already eliminated you. We next check your letters of reference. We consider who wrote the letters. Is the letter writer an academic? Are they your research supervisor? Do we know them? We evaluate how substantive they are, and if there are comparisons to other students (*i.e.*, does the letter state that you are as strong as another student who recently went to a top research university). We then look at your research statement, sometimes called a personal statement or statement of purpose (discussed in Chapter 7). We will sometimes arrange a phone interview with the applicant, and in some cases we will follow-up by phone with your references. Note that if we do not setup a phone interview it's not inherently a bad sign. We may arrange a phone interview to confirm the conclusion we've drawn from your application; but, sometimes the strength of the application is obvious and a phone call is unnecessary. This being said, we sometimes call strong applications to get them excited about our program and to answer any questions they may have. Finally, we look at everything else. In other words, we will look at every detail in your application, but we spend most of the time focusing on research-related experience.

You already know that your undergraduate research experience and letters of recommendation are two of the most important components of your application. We hear you saying "But what about my grades? They must be somewhat important too?" You're right, grades are important but they don't predict graduate school success nearly as well as undergraduate research experience or letters of recommendation. In terms of grades, we first confirm that you have good grades in "important" subjects. For a Computer Science graduate application, you should have done well in the core Computer Science courses. To us, that includes algorithms, data structures, theory of computation, relevant math courses (*e.g.*, discrete mathematics, probability), and any course specific to the research area in which you are applying. We also look to see if you've taken any advanced classes. For example, we like students who have done well in theory and machine learning, other faculty have different favorites. What grades correspond to having "done well"? For a top-tier grad program that means receiving an A- or better in the important courses. Sure, it's ok to have a few Bs, but if all your grades are B, we get concerned. If you consistently get Bs in the hard courses and As in the easy courses, we get concerned. Obtaining As in a few difficult courses likely indicates that if you are interested in a topic you can succeed. Since we expect you to select a research group and project that is interesting to you, we expect that you will do well. Your grades in "everything else" should be B- or better. If your grades aren't this strong, don't worry. We're describing what the very top schools are looking for (and of course there's no hard rule on this). If you have Bs and Cs but strong research experience you can still likely get into a graduate program – it's just not likely to be the top program.

Any terrible grades are red flags. That is, any Ds or Fs are likely to sink your application and need to be explained. Depending on the school to which you are applying, anything below a B- may also sink your application. What do we mean by "explained"? Well, say that you or a family member were very sick one semester and you spent a significant amount of time away from class. You can note this in your statement of purpose and we'll generally take it into consideration. We understand that things like this can happen. If your grades rebounded after the described event, that's great. As a word of caution, be honest about everything in your application. Keep in mind that if we know your letter writers we are likely to contact them for information beyond their letter of recommendation. Should a significant inconsistency be found between what's stated in your application and the truth, you will not be admitted.

A few final remarks. It is rarely the case that any one single faculty member has the authority to 'admit' a student against the wishes of the admissions committee. We mention this because every year we get countless emails from students asking us to directly admit them to our research groups. Our answer to all of them is the same, "we greatly appreciate your interest in joining our lab; however, you need to apply through the standard process and be accepted to the program by the admissions committee".

While some schools use waiting lists, it's important to realize that schools will not put students on a waiting list if they are not interested in having them join their department. Students placed on the waiting list are above the bar for admission to the school; however, there are other students being extended offers first. This could be because the students have stronger applications, or that their interests better fit research groups with openings.

While different institutions have their own protocols for review, the basic approach described above is the most common. From this, you can see the obvious fact that, the higher your GPA and test scores, the more likely your application will pass through the initial filtering steps and be matched with possible research groups. However, the further along your application gets, the less importance is given to your GPA and test scores. At later stages of evaluation, your research experience, letters of recommendation, and personal statement can make all the difference in gaining admission.

Note for Non-Native English Speakers

If you are not a native English speaker then we will also be looking on your application for signs that you can thrive at an English language university. The first thing we evaluate is your research statement. It's a bad sign if your research statement is written in broken English. If your research statement is written well we don't stop there – we know some students put significant effort into their research statement, solicit help from other English speakers, and use editing services. We will also look at the English in your resume, hints in the letters of recommendation, and your TOEFL score (if applicable). If we're still unsure we will likely try to get you on the phone for a conversational interview. The main point is, if you are not a native English speaker, make sure to demonstrate that you are proficient in English. We want every admitted student to succeed. It's not in our nor your best interest for you to come to an English language university and then struggle with the language for several years.

Chapter **6**

Where to Apply

It may seem obvious, but one of the most important decisions about graduate school is deciding where to apply. While this seems incredibly basic, we find that few students really take the time to mine the wealth of experience and advice around them before choosing a set of schools. More often than not, most prospective applicants simply choose from among the top-ranked schools (typically according to the latest U.S. News and World Report rankings), along with a safety school or two and hope for the best. In reality, rankings are just a small part of the equation; in this chapter we will discuss the important aspects of each graduate program that you should consider in addition to national rankings, and how to decide which programs fit your personal goals. Remember, unlike undergraduate admissions, when applying to graduate school you are essentially applying to a department and not the university as a whole. In the rest of this chapter, we focus on a few facets of a Ph.D. program (and of the university, when relevant) that will help you decide where to apply. We go into further detail on how to evaluate more specific aspects of a Ph.D. program after you've gained acceptance; see Chapter 9 ("Congrats, You've Been Admitted!") for that discussion.

Big versus Small Programs

Just like undergraduate institutions, graduate programs can vary greatly in size and scope of research areas. Consider for example, that the graduate programs at MIT EECS have nearly 890 students, 138 faculty (as of 2008) and graduates over a hundred Ph.D. students per year. In contrast, smaller, but still very highly regarded programs (such as Dartmouth), may be an order of magnitude smaller in scale. Large programs typically have the benefit of having a reputation for graduating students at a relatively even pace and of being of generally high quality in a large number of areas. In fact, you will often find that most of the schools in a particular science discipline that are ranked in the top ten are large, with hundreds of graduate students. In a large program, you will likely have the advantage that most research groups are fairly large, have plentiful resources and contain graduate students at different levels of experience along with postdoctoral researchers and even staff scientists. This type of research group can provide a level of camaraderie that is hard to find in a smaller setting. However, it is also the case that at a large program, you may have difficulty getting to know all the faculty, and you may at times find that a fair amount of coordination is required to meet with your own advisor. Smaller Ph.D. programs on the other hand, tend to excel in fewer research areas, and can provide the added benefit of a smaller community in which you may, for example, get to know nearly all of the faculty. In this setting you will more easily get the attention of your advisor and may even work side by side with him/her.

Another consideration is the availability of resources at a small versus large program. If you are seeking a Ph.D. in a discipline that requires considerable resources (*e.g.*, experimental physics) then you may want to bias your search toward larger institutions that are more likely to have the required resources. Of course, this is not set in stone. Small programs may have better or more modern resources than larger programs. There has also been a trend where multiple universities are beginning to share resources, putting both large and small schools on equal ground.

While we cannot list all of the pros and cons of small versus large programs here, suffice it to say that in the end, the choice depends primarily on your discipline and your personal preference for the type of environment that best suits you. For example, you may be attending a small liberal arts university and may be ready for a change. Or, if you are at a large institution, you may find that in your discipline, there are several small programs in which particular research groups are highly regarded and well-funded. As you consider schools in turn, keep in mind that there is no single best choice with respect to program size, and that often your own gut instinct can help you determine the short-list of programs to which you will apply.

Program Requirements

Each department's program requirements will dictate what is expected of you over the course of the degree. You will most often find this information in the "fine print" of program brochures or websites, but it is important to understand the specifics of course requirements, mentoring, and program milestones. Course requirements are perhaps the most uniform across programs in a particular discipline. Most typically, you will find about 2 years worth of required coursework (with about 3 courses per semester), take note if a particular program asks for much more coursework than this (Note: Biology and Chemistry departments tend to have fewer course requirements than Computer Science and Engineering). Ideally, you would like to have enough time to at least initiate a research project in the first year of coursework.

Mentoring and milestones tend to vary greatly from program to program, and we feel that this is an area that can make or break your progress through a Ph.D. degree. For example, a good rule of thumb is to check for at least one milestone per year. Programs that require only qualification exams or a research proposal and final defense tend to lose track of their students and can slow student progress. In contrast, programs that require early milestones, such as pre-qualification research projects, or required seminars that improve research and communication skills, help you focus your research topic and improve skills that can help you make progress in actually doing the research. Many programs also have requirements for teaching; for example, it is not uncommon to have one or two semesters in which you are required to be a teaching assistant (which may or may not include the presentation of lectures). If you are seeking an academic career, this is an excellent way to gain experience in the classroom. Too heavy a teaching load may of course hinder your progress. It is important to understand not only what the milestones are for any particular program, but also how the program is designed to help students meet these milestones. In general, most students do best when mentoring is provided early and often. Look for early mentoring; that is, can you choose a mentor upon entry, or must you complete certain requirements before you can select an advisor?

These subjective characteristics of how a program is administered are certainly hard to measure, but we have found that, the programs that make it easy for students to do research and that provide mentoring opportunities, often have happy and successful students. So perhaps the best way to understand whether a particular department is for you is to get in touch with students at various stages in that department. Often, departments will have a graduate student group whose purpose is to engage prospective and incoming students. Utilize this resource to understand how a program is run, whether students are happy, and how much of a voice students have in the program.

Research Strengths

As a graduate student your work will be focused in a particular research area. You will spend most of your time working with faculty and graduate students in that area. Because each program has different research strengths and weaknesses, it's best to identify your research interests before selecting where to apply. If you've participated in undergraduate research then you have an initial sense of at least one research area. If you're unsure what area most interests you, explore the options. Consider the courses that you found most fascinating. Read textbooks, journal articles, and websites. Talk with other undergraduate and graduate students. If your department has regular research seminars presented by local or visiting faculty (most do), attend the talks and see what piques your interest. Knowing your desired research area will influence where you apply. When considering schools, visit their websites and identify the faculty working in your area. Read about their research. The knowledge gained in this search will also be useful as you craft your Personal Statement (see Chapter 7).

Geographic Location

One generally overlooked aspect of a graduate program is its geographic location. In surveying the rankings, you will hardly ever find that this is a factor, primarily because it is so subjective. Of course mentoring, research groups, and camaraderie are important, but it is also important to make sure that your personal and social needs will be met. Consider if you prefer living in a large versus a small city. Do you want to be near other universities? Can you participate in social activities of interest? Where is the nearest airport? These are all personal decisions and there is no one correct answer. We can give you a general idea of where certain types of schools tend to be located; although this is the kind of rule that always has exceptions. Large public universities tend to have been established by a land-grant from the state and thus tend to be in more rural settings (*e.g.*, University of Illinois Urbana-Champaign, University of Michigan, University of Wisconsin Madison), although there are exceptions (University of California-Berkeley, University of Texas at Austin). Smaller private universities do tend to be somewhat in the vicinity of large cities (*e.g.*, Princeton, Harvard), although there are notable exceptions (*e.g.*, Dartmouth, Cornell).

Completion Time and Job Placement

From the student perspective, we believe that two very important criteria for measuring the quality of a Ph.D. program are completion time and job placement after graduation. At this early stage, it is fine to go by reported averages and statistics. For example, while the completion time for a Ph.D. depends on a number of factors, an average of 4 to 6 years is most reasonable in the sciences. Job placement statistics are also useful: determining whether graduates of a particular program preferentially join academia or industry can be an indicator of how well a program will fit your needs. These statistics are used for rankings, but are not always publicly available or advertised, and you may have to obtain them through the school's graduate program office. It is important to remember that these numbers may not tell the whole story. Once you are admitted, it will be very important to find out how quickly students in the research area or group that you will join make progress, and where they tend to go after graduation (see Chapter 9 for additional discussion).

Rankings

Now, let's consider how graduate programs are ranked. As it turns out, this question does not have a simple answer. A typical ranking scheme will take a variety of criteria, score each one numerically and combine the scores using some formula. There are usually a large number of criteria that go in to a numerical ranking, but usually the most heavily-weighted are: program size, number of faculty, program reputation, publications per faculty, funding per faculty, research awards and honors, and number of graduates per year. Perhaps the two most well-known rankings of graduate programs come from U.S. News and World Report (USNWR), a for-profit enterprise, and the National Research Council (NRC), a federal, non-profit group. These rankings differ in a number of important ways; we will discuss these differences and point out where we think these rankings are most useful.

Before we dive into discussing how the NRC and the USNWR rankings work, it is important to point out that these are by no means the only source of rankings. Professional organizations affiliated with scientific discipline often conduct their own surveys, and this information is likely to be very useful when comparing specific aspects of particular programs (*e.g.*, placement after graduation). As an example, in Computer Science the Computing Research Association (cra.org) is an excellent portal for such surveys. Similarly, the American Chemical Society (acs.org) contains many resources for Chemistry-affiliated disciplines. Finally it is also important to remember that, even though rankings are numerical in nature, it is often very difficult to meaningfully differentiate two programs that differ in only one or two places in their rankings. Programs with similar rankings will often differ in ways that are hard to evaluate numerically. Rankings are most useful when considered in larger increments, say groups of ten. That is, schools ranked 1-10 will generally be better than programs ranked 20-30, and so on.

The U.S. News and World Report rankings differ from the NRC

ranking in several ways. USNWR ranking are published yearly, and rely on a fixed formula that combines a number of criteria (described above) to determine the rank of each program. It is important to point out that while these criteria are more or less the same each year, their relative weights may be adjusted each year, and thus the USNWR rankings often change each year, since they are typically so close in score. Even though the USNWR rankings change slightly and are computed in a less than transparent manner, they are widely accepted as being a reasonable interpretation of the criteria. Also, the USNWR rankings provide ratings of particular research areas, for example in Computer Science, rankings are given for areas such as Artificial Intelligence, Systems, Theory, and so on. Thus they can be a good way to quickly identify a pool of schools that you may be interested in.

On the other hand, the National Research Council (NRC) evaluation of graduate schools are not even rankings per se. The NRC rates each graduate program on a number of criteria, and publishes the results without providing relative rankings. Unfortunately this is not done every year, or even every few years; the rankings have been published only every ten years or so in the form of a publication titled "A Data-Based Assessment of Research-Doctorate Programs in the United States". However, since the NRC is part of the National Academies, all of the detailed information of the NRC report is available at no expense. The most recent NRC report was published in 2010, and interestingly the data is available to browse free-of-charge in a format (at phds.org) that allows users to select their own weights for relative criteria. While the NRC rankings are quite transparent, a disadvantage is that they do not characterize the quality of research areas of any particular program. So, the NRC rankings may be a good way to relatively rank a pool of candidate programs that you have already identified.

Putting it All Together

Using the above criteria, you should determine a set of schools that best fits your personality, needs, and academic interests. Keep in mind that at this stage you are not committing to attend, you are simply applying. Only when you have your offers in hand do you have to finally decide. We feel it's important to not be swayed too much by any one factor (*i.e.,* don't apply to a school with a top ranking if everything else about the program isn't a good fit for you). We're often asked the number of schools to which each student should apply. Unfortunately this number changes from year to year, based on the number of applicants, openings, funding, etc. Our best advice is to ask current graduate students how many programs they applied to and to err on the side of applying to too many. It's better to have the problem of too many acceptances than too few. Finally, keep in mind that the top programs have lower acceptance rates, so if you're applying primarily to the strongest schools, you may want to consider applying more broadly.

Chapter 7

The Application

Your application materials are the sole interface between you and the admissions committees at the institutions to which you have applied. Each of these institutions will have hundreds to thousands of applicants to select from, and it is critical that your application materials play to your strengths. In this chapter, we will outline the contents of an application, describe the role of each component, and discuss how best to optimize your chances of admission.

What's in an Application?

Unlike an undergraduate application, which is evaluated primarily to determine whether you will succeed in the general environment of a university, a graduate application is much more specific. When an admissions committee evaluates an application to graduate school, the goal is to determine how well you will fit into their particular department, and even into a particular research group. To this end, you are asked to provide more detailed materials than in an undergraduate application. A graduate application most typically consists of: an academic transcript, standardized test scores (*i.e.*, Graduate Record Examinations, GRE), letters of reference, a personal statement, and a resume. Depending on your native language, you may also have to report TOEFL scores. Some programs also require a subject area GRE.

Letters of Reference

Once you have been flagged as at least a potential candidate for a Ph.D. program, your letters of reference will serve to solidify your record. The main role of these letters is to emphasize your unique strengths as they relate to success in a graduate program. In our experience, the primary mistake applicants make is to misjudge who would make a good letter writer. It's critical that the letters point to your initiative and enthusiasm for the research area you hope to pursue. In short, these letters should reinforce your academic transcript as well as your personal statement. They should illustrate your drive and passion for a particular area as well as your intellectual and creative abilities. You're likely to need at least three letters of recommendation. Because of the importance of the letters of reference, we have set aside the entire next chapter to discuss them in more detail.

Personal Statement

The second, and most malleable component of your graduate application is your personal statement. And yet, in our combined years on admissions committees, we have seen hundreds, if not thousands, of applications in which the personal statement was a boilerplate essay with lofty statements of passion and very few tangible reasons why the author should be admitted into our Ph.D. program. We have no doubt that these statements took the authors days if not weeks to craft; but, the effectiveness of such an approach is very limited. It is important to impress the admissions committee with a potent message of your research experience and interests.

So what should go into a personal statement? We prefer statements that focus on a particular research topic and describe how the applicant has taken concrete efforts to engage in that area (*i.e.*, undergraduate research experience, course projects, independent study, internships, etc.). Make your research statement interesting and attempt to engage or hook the reader. Strive to discuss the "cool factor" or why you are drawn to the research area. Describe one or two interesting technical details of your prior research or the research area you are interested in. Great personal statements leave the reader wanting to further engage with the author to continue the conversation. It's good if your personal statement connects with a faculty member or member of the admissions committee that can serve as your "champion." Unfortunately, there is no best way to write your personal statement – it is called a "personal" statement for a reason. Be sure to tie in your own experiences and ideas in a way that highlights your creative thought process and maturity. Remember that your statement will be read critically by experts with much more experience than you, so it pays to be humble in describing your aspirations.

We can suggest the following few simple guidelines to maximize the impact of your statement: keep it short, keep it specific, and don't fake it. The first guideline is obvious; we recommend a single page statement (unless the limit is shorter than this). Two pages may be ok, but anything over two pages is too long. Expositions of your family history or your personal passions should be kept fairly short. Instead, be as selective as possible about which personal or professional experiences you will cover in your personal statement. Your resume typically accompanies your application materials and will better serve as an exhaustive listing of your awards, honors and other accomplishments. In the personal statement, it is best to stick to the experiences that most directly support your desire to work in a particular area. Moreover, these experiences are most valuable in supporting your application if you can connect them to a tangible outcome, such as an award, a public presentation, or best of all, a publication. Given the space limitations of most personal statements, a good overall rule of thumb to follow is to focus on between one and three such experiences. It is worth pointing out that, while a scholarly product directly related to your interests will be a strong point of discussion, extracurricular activities (and accolades) can also be very useful in establishing the kind of graduate student, researcher, or teacher you are capable of becoming. If you are truly passionate about an activity, be sure that it plays to your strengths in your application.

The second guideline encourages you to keep the statement specific. Most of the discussion in your personal statement should be dedicated to specific reasons why you should be admitted to a particular program. Whether you focus on your own personal motivation for pursuing a general research area or on specific research interests, your research statement should be a statement of your "purpose" for being in the program to which you are applying. In other words, you should discuss not only your broad or specific goals, but also what you can add to a particular department, and how that clearly fits in with your overall career goals. It is best to explore these topics in very concrete terms. For example, it is worth spending time researching each department that you are applying to, taking note of which faculty work in the area(s) you are interested in. Then, tailor your personal statement for each program that you are applying to, connecting your interests and expertise to the relevant faculty and research groups.

The last guideline is to be realistic. It is a waste of time to inflate your experience or understanding of a particular topic or to be overly ambitious in stating research goals. Also, avoid overusing jargon or overly technical terminology. Realize that your application will most likely go to worldwide experts in various fields, and any false or naive statement in your area of interest will be met with disdain. It is far more valuable for the admissions committee to know how you can articulate interest or experience in the areas you know best, and identify the ways in which you wish to expand your knowledge in the future. Not only is the personal statement the best place to reinforce your strengths, but it is also a good setting to explain perceived shortcomings in an honest and positive way.

In addition to these guidelines, you should be very careful about typographical and grammatical errors. These kinds of mistakes can be easily fixed, and submitting a personal statement with typos shows a general lack of care on the part of the applicant. Give your final draft of the personal statement an extra read-through to ensure that it is as polished as possible.

We've covered several important guidelines for writing your personal statement. But how do you know if it will pass muster and "hook" the admissions committee or a potential faculty advisor? Unfortunately, you cannot revise your application once it has been submitted; you will not get an opportunity to make clarifications about your academic record, or edit your personal statement. A good way to ensure that your personal statement "works" is to simply ask a faculty member in your department to look it over. If you are in a department that has a Ph.D. program, consider approaching a member of the graduate admissions committee in your current department. You can typically find a representative of the graduate admissions committee through your department's graduate office. If you are at an institution or department without a graduate program, a faculty member that is also one of your letter-writers would be an excellent choice to review your personal statement. Of course, be sure to give these folks plenty of time. Given that many deadlines are in late fall, try to have your application ready in early fall. At least in the semester system, faculty are often quite busy the first few weeks of class and will likely take at least that much time to give you feedback.

Following our suggestions will differentiate your personal statement from hundreds of others that are an unfortunate combination of poetic prose and lofty goals. Again, keep it short, be specific, and don't fake it. As a final caveat, we remind you that a personal statement cannot really be written in a week or two. It will take you more time than you think to focus your thoughts, and to produce a statement that is clear and to the point. Unlike written assignments in your classes, the graduate school application is an all-or-nothing proposition. It is your one and only chance to provide admissions committees an insight into your motivations and goals, and it is worth your time to get it right. Give yourself at least 3-4 weeks to produce a first draft, and then at least another two weeks to rework the statement after getting feedback as we discuss above.

Resume

An academic resume (*i.e.,* curriculum vitae, or CV as it is often called) is sometimes a requirement for a graduate school application. If you need to include a resume, it is important to realize that it is somewhat different than a resume you may have used in the past to apply for non-academic positions. When evaluating an academic resume, admissions committees usually focus more on academic experience and background than on specific job skills. Be sure to highlight research experience and list research interests. In most cases, your resume will contain most of the following sections: Education, Awards/Honors, Research Experience, Work Experience, Teaching Experience, Publications/Presentation Extracurricular and Service Activities, and Skills. It's worth mentioning that in the extracurricular activities section you should focus on activities that are relevant to your application (*i.e.*, peer mentoring, academic contests and clubs). Overall, it pays to keep your resume short and to avoid repetition; for example, it is usually unnecessary to list coursework since it is part of your transcript. It should serve as a quick fact sheet that can be consulted when your personal statement and letters of reference are being reviewed. A good rule of thumb is to limit your CV to one or two pages. Your resume should only be longer if you have worked on multiple research projects and have a sizable number of publications.

A Word on Fellowships

As a part of the process of applying to graduate school, you should also consider seeking financial support that is independent of any particular school. Funding for graduate work can come from a variety of public and private organizations (*e.g.*, Microsoft, IBM, NSF, NIH). These sources typically offer graduate students 2-4 years of full support for graduate work. You can typically obtain a listing of available fellowships from the professional organization connected to your discipline. Many government-based fellowships are listed at grants.gov.

Fellowships are often competitive because of a large applicant pool, and require an application that is somewhat similar to a graduate school application. This is certainly extra work, but if you can apply and secure a fellowship prior to submitting your application you can often improve your chances of being admitted. Having external funding for a Ph.D. makes applicants very attractive to prospective departments for two reasons. First and foremost, it provides a validation of your skills and abilities. Second, it allows a department greater flexibility in choosing Ph.D. students, since you can be admitted to a department without a funding commitment (aside from perhaps a tuition waiver). Last but not least, do not wait until after you have applied to graduate programs to begin your fellowship applications. Many fellowship applications are due *before* graduate school applications. So don't wait to complete your graduate school applications to begin your fellowship applications. Ideally, you should finish your fellowship applications first and use that experience to more effectively complete your graduate school applications.

Interviews

Although not part of your formal application materials, it's worth mentioning that some schools interview candidates as part of their evaluative process. Interviews are arranged after admissions committees have eliminated the least promising students from consideration. In other words, if you receive an interview you are near or above the bar for admission. A strong interview will make the case for you to be admitted. Interviews are more common in the basic sciences (*i.e.,* Chemistry, Biology, Biochemistry) and are less common in Engineering and Computer Science. Engineering and Computer Science tend to invite admitted students for a 'visit day' where schools try to convince you to choose them. Interviews and interview visits are actually mutual – that is, while they are interviewing you, you are also deciding if you want to attend their program. We tell you how to get the most out of a visit day in Chapter 9 and we encourage you to read that section in preparation for both visit days and interviews.

Interviews can be conducted both in-person and over the phone. Phone interviews tend to be quick (15-60 minutes) and conducted by one or two faculty. In-person interviews tend to take place on campus. They consist of several one-on-one faculty meetings, meetings with graduate students, several social events, as well as lab, department, and campus tours. It goes without saying that you want to make your best impression during an interview. Therefore it's obviously worth preparing before the interview starts. If you know with whom you will meet, try to obtain some background information on their academic interests. If you don't know who you are going to meet, try to make an educated guess based on research interests. Interview days can be long and tiring. Be sure to get a good night's sleep before the interview. Use caffeine as necessary (but don't over caffeinate). Be sure to drink lots of liquids (you'll get dry talking and drinking caffeine). If you have scheduled downtime through the day, make good use of it. Just sit, grab a snack, chat with people. When the day is over, be sure to send a quick follow-up email to thank the people you met with. If you told anyone that you would follow-up by sending them a paper or link, do so.

In terms of questions you might be asked, be sure you have answers to all the following: Why did you decide to attend graduate school? Why do you want to attend our university? What are your primary research interests? What are your strengths? What are your weaknesses? Who in our department would be the best fit for your research interests? Can you tell me about your undergraduate research experience? Can you tell me about a particularly challenging issue with your research and how you solved it? You should also prepare for a few more 'sticky' questions (you're not likely to be asked these but you should prepare in case they come up): Where else are you applying? What schools are your top choices? Who would you want to work with if you came here? In addition, be sure you can discuss perceived weaknesses on your application if they happen to come up in conversation.

When we meet with a potential student we're trying to gauge their fit with our lab by using the criteria we've discussed above. We first try to establish some rapport with the student by talking about something non-technical. This could be about the weather, sports, or where they're from. Then we jump into research. We ask what they're most interested in and why. Using their CV as a guide, we ask a few questions about their recent research projects. Be sure to brush up on your work before the interview. It does not look good if you can't answer detailed questions about your research. Review the methods that you used, why you selected them, and of course be able to clearly explain the details of why you did what you did. Why was the project important? Why was the project interesting? Why was the project difficult? We're looking to see if you can explain your work and determine if you really understood what you did. We'll then transition into talking about research in our lab. We may pick an interesting problem we're working on or something that's just neat to discuss. We'll lay out the problem and then ask your thoughts. We don't expect you to solve the research problem during the interview - likely the problem is difficult and you are seeing it for the first time. We are looking to see that you are ask good questions and that you are approaching the problem in a reasonable way. We're also looking to make sure you understand what we're explaining to you.

Our advice wouldn't be complete without a list of things to avoid. While you should appear calm and confident you should make every effort to not come across as arrogant. This is one of the top two reasons why people 'fail' interviews (the other reason being lack of intellectual proficiency). If you are a genius but you come across as arrogant you may not pass the interview. The reason is that the school and research group has to work with you for 4-6 years and they do not want to work with a jerk. Avoiding coming across as arrogant is often more difficult than it sounds. While you know you shouldn't intentionally insult people, you do want to convince your interviewer that you are smart. If you repeatedly demonstrate your knowledge, it might come across as showing-off. There are three tricks to demonstrating your knowledge but not coming across as arrogant. First, don't interrupt others (other students or the interviewer) to demonstrate your knowledge. Wait until it makes sense to answer. Second, in a group setting don't be the one who answers the most questions. You can be the person who answers the second most number of questions and let the other guy look like a show-off. Finally, avoid saying anything negative – about anything. Don't say anything negative about a person, a method, a research topic, a city, a university, etc. You never know how others feel about these things. If you really feel negative about something, it's best to take a more neutral stance.

So in summary, during an interview you want to do your homework and prepare to ensure good discussions with your interviewers. You want to appear friendly and outgoing while avoiding arrogance, and you want to follow-up with the people you've met. There are many books dedicated to the art of interviewing and we certainly cannot do the topic complete justice in a single section. We encourage you to utilize other resources and talk with students who have gone on interviews. If you can find a local faculty or graduate student who is willing to give you a mock interview, practice with them. If you receive multiple interview requests, you may want to schedule them so that your top-choice school is not your first interview. This way, you'll have experience by the time you interview at your top-choice program.

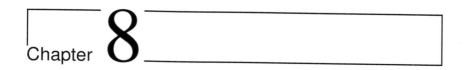

Chapter 8

Letters of Reference

We've said it several times: the most important message your application can convey is that you have what it takes to make an intellectual contribution to a research lab. We mentioned that the admissions committee uses several pieces of information to determine this, the most important of which is likely to be your letters of reference. If you have a strong letter from someone both known and respected by the admissions committee, you'll be in great shape. But what else makes or breaks a letter of recommendation? In this chapter we'll first discuss who writes the most influential letters, then we'll give you advice on how to go about asking for a strong letter. We'll provide detail on what you should be doing to maximize the impact of the letter. However, we should warn you now, there's no magic bullet. If you're not a strong student, there's no magic phrase to utter to obtain a golden recommendation. We'll simply help you get the best set of recommendations you possibly can.

When the admissions committee looks at a letter they look at three things: 1) who wrote the letter, 2) how well the letter writer knows you, and 3) what the letter says about you. The first point validates the letter writer, the second point validates that they can say something about you, and the third point is the actual message.

Who Writes the Best Letters?

We're going to ignore the content for a moment and just focus on the person writing the letter. Broadly speaking, when evaluating applications, we pay most attention to letters from academic faculty who have supervised your research. Ranking second are letters from academic faculty from whom you've taken courses. Ranking a distant third are letters from industry (unless the letter is from a Ph.D. in an industrial research lab – which would bump the importance of the letter up to that of an academic faculty from whom you've taken a course). Least significant are letters from community or religious leaders. Letters from teaching assistants or postdocs are difficult to interpret. Most of these students are less experienced letter writers and tend to provide glowing, but uninformative, letters. Why is this the priority we place on letters of reference? It comes back to two things: 1) what the letter tells us about your ability to function in an academic research environment and 2) the trustworthiness of the reference. So ideally, you'd have worked with the three top faculty in your research area and you would have letters from them stating that you are the next Einstein. That's not likely to happen. And that's ok.

Why is it so much better to get a letter from a well-known research professor? These individuals have significant experience and know which students are likely to be successful in a research career. These faculty are also less likely to throw around inflated recommendations. If they recommend a student and the student turns out to not be as impressive as they claimed, then it reflects poorly on the faculty. Ideally such a letter will compare your abilities to other students with whom they have worked and who have gone on to be successful. For example, "In summary, Joe's overall research ability is similar to two of my previous students who have gone on to successful graduate careers at University X" (where University X is a good school).

Who should you ask for a recommendation? There is no perfect formula. Some students can easily find two letter writers, but struggle with the third. Others have more than three possibilities and struggle to determine which three to choose. Get letters from faculty that you've worked with (*i.e.*, people that really know you). Here's an ideal approach, which is unfortunately not going to work for very many people. Get two strong letters from your undergraduate research supervisors and get a third letter from a very well-known faculty member in your department from whom you've taken a class, done well, and gotten to know outside the lecture hall. If you have these three then skip down to the section on how to ask for letters, otherwise read on.

Hopefully you have at least one of the three letters we just described. Ideally this is from your undergraduate research supervisor. In fact, if you've participated in undergraduate research, then you must get a letter from the faculty supervising your research. Why? Well, you're going to mention your undergraduate research and so the admissions committee is going to look for a letter from your advisor. If you don't have one, they will wonder why. There are three possibilities: 1) you never asked, 2) you asked, but they declined, or 3) they simply forgot to send it in. Because (3) is unlikely, we're going to assume that the reality is either (1) or (2), both of which imply that your supervisor would not have provided a strong letter.

If you still need more letters, walk down the list (from a few paragraphs back, well known faculty, lesser known faculty, course instructors, and finally industry or teaching assistants). Weight each letter by how strong the letter will be and how well they know you. There may be a very well known professor in your department, but if they don't really know you then it's not worth asking for a letter. As you'll see below, you want the letter to give specific examples supporting your strengths.

Non-North American Letters of Reference

As we've stated, letters of reference are most useful when they come from someone we know. Quite frequently we do not know most faculty at non-North American universities. Non-North American letter writers are typically not as familiar with the letter writing process and they have a tendency to provide short, glowing, but uninformative, letters. In other words, they are not terribly helpful. If you are applying from a non-North American school, it's beneficial to get at least one of your letters from a faculty-member at a North American university. This is a good reason to attempt to collaborate with someone in North America or to do an internship here.

The Contents of a Reference Letter

Remember that one goal of the letter is to convince the admissions committee that you will be successful in a research program. Your letter writers must be able to make strong superlative statements and should provide supporting evidence for each statement. For example, rather than simply saying, "Joe is a problem solver", a better letter will give an example of the time Joe found a creative solution to a problem faced by another member of the lab. For example, that Joe had the idea, followed up by reading the appropriate primary research literature, and presented a solution in group meeting. This is why you may want to remind your letter writers about these events when they agree to write a reference. As we detail below, it is often a good idea to have an initial draft of your application materials (resume, transcript, personal statement) to give to your letter writers, so they have information from which to work.

Strong versus Weak Letters

It is unlikely that you will receive an overtly weak letter of reference. If a letter writer can't find anything positive to say they will not accept your request for them to write a letter. So how do we interpret letters if none of them are obviously weak? We have adopted an unwritten code of sending secret messages in our letters. Well, of course it's not really that sinister. If a letter only says "Joe showed up to lab meeting and did what was asked of him," we interpret that as a sign of mediocrity.

We are instead looking for specific examples of greatness, supported by incident-based evidence.

Asking for a Reference Letter

You know who you want to ask, but how should you go about asking them? It's best to ask in person. Faculty receive so much email that yours may get lost in the pile. Regardless of if you are currently taking their class, stop in during their office hours. If you are working in a research lab, you likely already have a regular meeting when you can bring up the subject. Tell your potential letter writer that you are currently applying to graduate schools. Ask them if they would feel comfortable writing a "strong letter of recommendation". This phrasing allows the letter writer to gracefully turn you down if they are only able to write a mediocre letter. That is, if they agree to writing a strong letter of reference, they generally will do so. If you sense any reluctance to your request, if they say "maybe" or "I could write a letter but maybe you would be able to get a stronger letter from someone with whom you've worked more closely", then you should thank them for the advice and move on to someone else. Do not go back to them for a letter unless you have no choice or there are other extenuating circumstances. You want your letter writer to reply "Certainly, I would be very happy to write you a strong reference letter."

Once your letter writer has agreed to write a reference, you should provide them with several resources to facilitate their letter writing. You should provide an updated copy of your resume and transcript, your personal statement, and a reminder of the work you did together (*i.e.*, which courses and what semester). If you received a particularly high mark on a course project you could remind them of the project details. You can also gently ask if they wouldn't mind focusing on some particular aspect of your application. What we mean is, a faculty from whom you've taken a class can focus on your classroom abilities (perhaps also oral presentation or leadership strengths) but shouldn't be asked to deeply discuss your research (they don't know it). Overall, consider the types of messages you want each letter writer to convey and provide supporting evidence to allow them to write such a letter.

Make the process as easy as possible for the letter writers. If the recommendation needs to be completed on a special form, you should fill out as much of the form as possible before giving it to your letter writer (*i.e.*, your name, address, etc.). If the letters need to be mailed in, you should provide your letter writers addressed stamped envelopes.

This way, the letter writer only needs to write and print your letter. If you are asking your letter writer to send the letter to multiple schools, you should provide an organized checklist of schools that includes due dates.

Although you don't want to annoy your letter writers, you can send a gentle reminder email when it's a week or two before the deadline. You can simply check in to ask if they've sent the letter. If the deadline passes and the school tells you that you are missing references, you should of course gently let the letter writer know about this.

A Few Final Notes

Be sure to give your letter writers plenty of time. Ideally four weeks or more. You want to provide them enough time to write a strong letter without being rushed. Many letter writers will have to prepare letters for dozens of students. They can't do all of them overnight. If you give the letter writer very little time, their potential frustration with the timeframe could be reflected in the quality of the letter.

People forget – although your sophomore or junior research supervisor is not going to forget you after a year, they may not easily be able to recall situational examples of when you excelled in the lab. These are the types of examples you want them to include in the reference letter. So, it's a good strategy to ask for a letter as soon as you are finished working with a faculty member. In other words, if you are only a sophomore or junior and you know you are not going to have any additional major interaction with this professor, you can ask them to prepare (and hold) a letter or letter draft while you are still a sophomore or junior. Then, when you are ready to apply, you can ask the professor if he/she would still be willing to submit that letter, perhaps updated with a few things that have happened since. Note that in most cases you should not do this as a freshman. It's too early. One, you likely weren't as impressive as you think and two, even if you are good, the chance of you actually using that letter above all the others you can obtain in your second and third years is small. So only ask for letters from faculty when you think you will use the letter later on. It's extremely frustrating to be asked to spend an hour or two preparing a reference letter for a student only to learn that they aren't going to use the letter after all.

You should not ask to read or review your letter. Most North American schools require the letters to be confidential. If the letter writer offers to share the letter with you, our advice is to politely decline. You can say that you'd like all your letters to be confidential. Most schools accept reference letters through an online system. If there is an option (*i.e.*, electronic versus paper) you should give that choice to your letter writer. While electronic submission is often efficient, some faculty prefer to use paper because the online systems are often poorly designed. Finally, be sure to thank your letter writers. Nothing fancy, just a brief email or short thank you in person. People appreciate being appreciated.

Chapter 9

Congrats! You've Been Admitted!

Congratulations are in order – your hard work has paid off and you've gained admission to a number of Ph.D. programs. If you're lucky, you've been admitted to more than one program and you must now make a choice. You must decide which institution will be your intellectual home for the next 4-6 years. Throughout the application process, your exposure to each Ph.D. program has been quite indirect. While you may have spoken to people familiar with each institution or their faculty, you have probably relied on second-hand information. Now that you have gained admission into one or more programs, you must investigate the details.

It is important to understand how a program supports graduate students and ensures steady progress through the Ph.D. program. Only some schools and disciplines conduct graduate school interviews during which applicants learn about the program, but most departments will offer a 'prospective student' or 'visit' day to woo admitted students (discussed later in this chapter). If you've been admitted to a number of programs, try and narrow your options to two or three programs to visit. Participating in a visit day requires a fair amount of time, but provides the best opportunity to get more information about each program. Departments often put their best face forward during the visit day, and it is thus easy to be seduced by their facilities or a few select research projects. In the rest of this chapter, we will cover a few topics that will help you better understand how a Ph.D. program can be organized, what to look for to ensure your progress and success, and the questions you should ask when you have the opportunity to visit the department.

As a side note, if you haven't heard back from all of the programs to which you have applied, it is important to point out that there is not a strict schedule of acceptance dates for graduate programs. If you have not heard from a program, be proactive in contacting the department. Having been on admissions committees, we can tell you that it is often a somewhat bureaucratic process to officially contact accepted students. When contacting a graduate program, politely let them know your deadlines and the date by which you'd like to know whether you have been accepted into their program. Typically, after receiving an official acceptance letter you will need to inform programs of your decision by early- to mid-April.

Funding

You may know that Ph.D. students receive tuition waivers and monthly stipends. But where does this money come from, and how is your tuition to the graduate program covered? Most typically, tuition is covered in full for Ph.D. students either by the department or university in the form of a tuition waiver. Funding for stipends, typically including health benefits, can be provided by the department, research grants to principal investigators, or fellowships provided by federal, non-profit, or private agencies. Administratively, the funding (regardless of source) comes in the form of a *teaching assistantship* (TA) or a *research assistantship* (RA). For example, you may receive a teaching assistantship in exchange for helping a professor teach an undergraduate course; as a TA, you would have the same responsibilities as the TAs of your current courses (imagine that). Through most of your graduate career you will be supported on a research assistantship for doing the routine research activities of a graduate student. Some departments will automatically consider you for 'special' fellowships upon admission.

As discussed in Chapter 7 ("The Application"), admission to a program may be connected to a particular faculty that serves as your research advisor, or it may be extended generally with the expectation that you select an advisor in the first year. In the latter scenario, the ideal situation is of course that every Ph.D. student is given a fellowship upon admission. If this is not the case, you must determine whether you will be eligible for department funding during the time you are choosing an advisor. A good program will often prioritize teaching assistantships for incoming Ph.D. students.

For programs in which you are assigned to a particular faculty member, it is very important to see how funding tied to a faculty member affects your progress through the degree. For example, if you join a research group and then choose to change advisors, is the department willing to provide a teaching assistantship until you can obtain a research assistantship with the new lab? A good program will ensure that funding is as decoupled as possible from progress through the requirements for the degree.

It is also important to look at the big picture when evaluating the financial health of a graduate program. That is, how many Ph.D. students are unsupported and how many rely on teaching assistantships (rather than research assistantships or external fellowships)? Consider how far along these students are in their degree. These questions are important, because it indicates the level of funding that the department is capable of, and how well it is able to make up for "slack" in funding of particular research projects. It is often the case that researchers have projects that are pending funding, and departments that can easily provide a semester or two of teaching assistantship support are well-prepared to deal with the vagaries of research funding. In a research-active department, you generally expect to see the majority of students funded by research grants or fellowships. Unfunded students should be the exception rather than the rule.

As a final note, the actual amount of funding should also be considered, but should be a second-order issue. Programs that offer funding generally try to match other institutions, and many federal funding agencies prescribe minimum (and maximum) amounts for student support. In some programs, department fellowships may provide for a higher level of support than teaching or research assistantships.

Departmental Requirements

As mentioned in Chapter 6 ("Where To Apply"), a critically important part of your progress through your Ph.D. is how you transition into a research role. Overall, you should be asking what the concrete program requirements are in the first 2 years to determine whether there a good balance of requirements for coursework and research. Programs that involve new students in research within the first or second semesters often have more success in retention and graduation. Moreover, it is ideal if this approach is part of actual degree requirements; for example, through a required seminar course in the first year in which you choose (or are assigned) a mentor with whom you must do a small project.

Also consider how many total courses and degree checkpoints are required to complete the program. Most universities have multiple checkpoints to ensure steady progress. One of the earliest are qualification or comprehensive exams. These are oral or written tests used to demonstrate a students breadth and depth of knowledge. Dont worry about these now, but its good to know they exist and to familiarize yourself with the general policy for their completion.

Finally, learning to teach is an important component of obtaining a Ph.D., particularly if your career goal is to obtain an academic position. While research presentations and the general process of doing research is a great way to learn to teach, it is also ideal if a program has a mechanism for providing teaching experience, as well as a way to impart teaching skills (ideally a required course) to graduate students. Be sure to determine how many semesters (if any) of teaching assistantships (TAs) are required and if you will have the opportunity to gain in-class teaching experience.

Joining a Research Group

This is perhaps the most variable practice among different departments and disciplines. In the life sciences, this choice is very structured: there is a well established "rotation" model of finding an advisor, in which students spend the first year or two essentially trying out different labs each semester. Typically students are given three rotations to determine which lab is the best fit for their career goals, and at the end of three rotations must choose and agree to be accepted by a particular research lab. In other disciplines that do not emphasize lab work, this model is quite rare, so it is all the more important to find out what the typical process is for identifying and working with a dissertation advisor. You should determine the process for joining a research lab at each program you are considering, and you should also determine how actively the department enables or facilitates this process.

As mentioned earlier, there are essentially two styles of admission, and these of course affect how you will be able to join a lab, as well as how you easily you will be able to transition between labs if necessary. In the best-athlete model, you will likely have a provisional or interim advisor assigned as you enter the program. It is important to find out (from both students and faculty) how quickly students transition from their interim advisor to their dissertation advisor. In some departments you will join the research group of the faculty member who has agreed to advise and fund you. This is in fact a very common practice, and you should not take this type of admission to mean that you are not allowed to consider any other research group. Instead, we think this model can provide a smooth transition to doing dissertation research. However, if you do decide to switch groups, it is very important to talk to students and faculty to understand how easily this can be done. Again, the department should have a clear and reasonable policy in place for such changes, and ideally would provide funding (likely in the form of a teaching assistantship) to "bridge" this change from one advisor to another.

Finally as we alluded to in "Where to Apply" (Chapter 6), departments, as well as research groups, can be large or small. Once you have been admitted either to work with a particular faculty member, or to a department in general, you should take note of the size and composition of research groups. First, and foremost, do some background work on research groups in your area(s) of interest. Pay attention to the size and productivity (in terms of publications) of these candidate groups. In larger research groups, students often work on one large project together, being responsible for individual components of a sizable research problem. In this type of setting, a research group that works well together will be motivated and able to tackle and make progress on large research problems. During your visit, you should try to determine whether the group you are considering runs in this ideal manner. Also, will you be able to meet with the head of this large research group on a regular basis? How well do other students in the lab interact with one another, and your potential advisor? If you have not been assigned an advisor upon admission, then you should more broadly survey the department and try to ascertain which groups in your interest area(s) work together best (*i.e.*, produce high-quality publications, obtain research funding, and graduate Ph.D.s at regular intervals). If you will be working in a smaller research group, then it is important to ensure you will receive the mentoring you need to make progress. Does your potential advisor have projects that you could work on, and more importantly, do you think you could get along with him or her?

Department Health

The administration of a Ph.D. program is critical to your success, but of equal importance is the way in which the department is organized. In particular, there are several important aspects of a department, namely the faculty composition, overall student community and attitude, and departmental facilities that will affect your success in research during your Ph.D.

An important consideration in assessing the general "health" of a department is the extent to which research groups communicate and collaborate. We often find that departments with highly collaborative environments often have a certain energy and buzz that create an exciting environment for everyone. Collaboration between research groups in the department is evidence of a number of positive attributes. First, it shows that faculty are open to new ideas and to building teams of researchers to attack a particular problem. This in turn creates an environment that is very rich from the student's perspective, because they learn to think and communicate research ideas in a fairly broad way. Second, collaborative efforts often have a higher chance of receiving funding and making research progress. Finally, and perhaps most importantly, students in the right collaborative environment often have a better experience in mentoring and being mentored, simply because there are more students, postdoctoral researchers, and faculty available. It is relatively rare, of course, that a department has the best of all worlds, and to some extent the best environment differs for each individual. It is important to point out that even if there is not a high degree of active collaboration between groups, we find that departments that encourage engagement between research groups, for example in journal clubs and seminar series, often have a sense of excitement about research. Rather than checking off a list of the above attributes, your goal should instead be to see if there is a sense of excitement among faculty, and if the level of communication and collaboration in the department (or a research group) "feels" like it would be a constructive atmosphere for you. Moreover, it can also help you choose among research groups if you are considering more than one area of research.

As a graduate student, it is a given that you will be spending most of your time around other students, be it in the classroom, the lab, or in a social setting. Thus it important to get an idea of whether the graduate student community in your prospective department will be conducive to your progress. While your expectations will be informed by your own experience (*i.e.,* depending on your undergraduate department), in general you should look for some kind of graduate student community. The best evaluation of this will be from your visit; you should seek to talk to students at different points in their degree and assess how much they interact with their cohort. In our opinion, a good student community fosters easy communication and socialization. For example, spontaneous discussions of research problems, whether in the graduate lounge or at a party, are often a good sign that students are happy with what they are doing.

While the above discussion is mostly subjective, there are also a few important objective criteria to evaluate during your visit. First, how mixed is the student population in terms of degree progress? A roughly even distribution of students' entry time into the program indicates a fairly steady rate of recruitment, as well as a fairly steady rate of graduation. You should take note of this both at the departmental level as well as in the research groups you are interested in. A related statistic to also take note of is the average completion time of students. An average completion time of about five years shows that the program requirements and faculty are both working to help students complete their degrees in a timely manner. If the completion time of a program is much longer, regardless of the ranking, this indicates a potential problem with mentoring policies.

You should also evaluate where students are placed after graduation; this is one of the key measures of success of a Ph.D. program. In some research areas (*e.g.*, computational biology, machine learning), it is common to do a stint as a postdoctoral researcher, and in others (*e.g.*, systems) a good industrial research position is a sign of success. It is important to identify the criteria for success in your particular research area, and examine the outcomes for the program you are interested in. It is also important to remember that not all schools do well in placing graduates in both academia and industry. It may very well be the case that certain schools are very successful at academic placement, while others tend to emphasize and succeed at industrial positions. One good way to evaluate this particular aspect of a program is on the prospective student visit day (discussed below).

Finally, an important aspect of a graduate department is the infrastructure and facilities that will be available to you. Of course, your particular discipline will dictate the large or small equipment that may be necessary for your research; your visit will be an ideal time to talk to students and faculty to see if research-specific equipment needs are being met. Be sure to talk with current Ph.D. students to determine the adequacy of shared lab and computing resources. For example, are most entering students provided a "work" computer? Also, if you have been admitted to a particular research lab or group, it is important to determine which resources are shared with other groups; try to assess how much, if any, competition there is for shared resources. More generally, however, you should also assess the workspace that you will likely have. For example, are all students provided with a dedicated workspace, regardless of whether they are being funded? Are the workspaces close to critical equipment, or to other members of your research group, including your advisor? This is somewhat subjective as well, but you should feel that the facilities available to you provide easy access to your advisor, research group, any other resources you may need.

Visit Day

So you've armed yourself with questions and observations to prepare for an in-person visit of the department you've been accepted to. To ensure good participation in these visits, most departments will subsidize, or completely pay for, travel and accommodation. If your department does not hold such an event, then you may want to arrange a visit yourself, by getting in touch with the admissions committee and relevant faculty.

In general, visits to a prospective department are generally short and well organized with a mix of presentations and one-to-one meetings with faculty. If you are given your schedule ahead of time, it is a good idea to do your homework on the faculty you will meet. Check out their webpages and familiarize yourself with their research and recent projects. This will allow you to make a great impression and is a first step to helping you join a lab should you end up at that university. To get the most out of other visit day activities you should formulate a set of questions relating to aspects of the program that are most important to you. Questions about program organization will likely be answered best during the period of the visit when the department chair (or graduate program head) provides an overview of the graduate program. Typically there is also a period where faculty members provide brief overviews of their research groups and current projects. This is likely the best time to get an overall idea of the level of communication and collaboration between research groups. Most visit days also incorporate some kind of social activity with faculty and students. This is one of the best ways to get a handle on the health of the graduate student community and the overall social atmosphere. While we hesitate to call it "networking" with faculty and graduate students, it most certainly pays to be outgoing and friendly in any and all social settings. If, after the visit day activities are over, you have the opportunity to have a drink or a meal with students, faculty or other prospective students, you should take advantage of it. It is not uncommon for scientists to have the best ideas in the most unlikely of places, and by being outgoing you may get answers to questions you didn't think of, or a new perspective on a research group or the department in general.

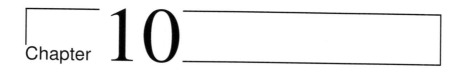

Chapter **10**

You Didn't Get In, Now What?

The previous chapter assumes that you have been fortunate enough to be offered admission into a program of your choice. But, what should you do if you didn't receive any acceptances? First, don't take it personally. The admissions process is imperfect. You'll simply try again to match your application to a program that fits. Try to identify any academic weaknesses (*e.g.*, lower than expected grades in a particular area), that can be addressed with additional coursework, extracurricular study, or work experience. It may also be a good idea to approach your letter writers for advice in this regard. Ask if there is any particular area you could work on to improve your application or strengthen their recommendation.

In most of this book, we've emphasized that research experience is the single best thing you can do to strengthen your application. If you didn't receive an acceptance, a good move is to bolster your application with more research experience. For example, in the life sciences, it is very common for college graduates to take up a lab technician or staff position in a research group even before applying to graduate school. Such staff positions are fairly common in any sizable research group, and are often advertised via the discipline's professional organization. Not only can this type of position give you an intimate look at the inner workings of a research group, it also provides the opportunity to find out about the types of research projects you may work on as a Ph.D. student. Moreover this type of position can help you develop a relationship with the leader of the research group, so that when you apply again to Ph.D. programs you can have another strong, focused letter of recommendation.

Working in a research lab also exposes you to a range of activities that can improve your knowledge of your discipline, and inspire interest in particular research problems. With the opportunity for hands on experience also come opportunities to attend seminars by visiting researchers and to participate in journal clubs. Also try your best to contribute ideas to your lab's research projects. If your ideas help a project succeed, you may have the opportunity to attend a conference with other lab members. Scientific meetings are one of the primary means of communicating scientific research results, and in a sense this is where it all happens. If you are lucky enough to attend a scientific conference before applying to graduate school, you will have the opportunity to see high-quality scientific lectures, but also real scientific interaction between attendants during meals and poster sessions. During the meeting you should also seek out faculty from programs where you wish to apply. If you made a good impression, the faculty will likely remember the interaction if they are asked to evaluate your application.

Even if you are not working in a research lab, it is not difficult to improve your breadth of knowledge in the most current scientific research. To follow the "big" trends, each month try to read articles from Nature, Science, or one or two journals in areas of your interest. Take the initiative to learn about new research problems and areas as the opportunities arise. Also, many cities have multiple universities in close proximity. If you have access to seminar series being conducted at a local university (or perhaps the one at which you are working), this is an excellent way to stay connected to the scientific research community.

By taking just an hour or two each week to do these things, you will gain breadth of knowledge in your discipline that will serve you well when the time comes to reapply to graduate school. You will likely find that you can rework your personal statement to reflect the maturity and breadth of knowledge that you have gained. Moreover, you will be able to talk competently about your areas of interest and perhaps even cite relevant papers.

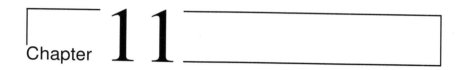

Chapter **11**

Starting Out

So at this point the long application process is complete. Either that or you're simply reading ahead in excited anticipation of what will soon be. We're only going to devote a single chapter to graduate school success because there are a number of excellent books on the topic. As a next step, we recommend three books, "The Ph.D. Process: A Student's Guide to Graduate School in the Sciences" by Bloom, Karp, and Cohen; "Getting What You Came For: The Smart Student's Guide to Earning an M.A. or a Ph.D." by Peters; and "A Ph.D. is Not Enough!: A Guide to Survival in Science" by Feibelman (the last book is good for students close to finishing their thesis).

We spent a lot of time discussing the key pieces of an application indicative of a student that will be successful in graduate school. We mentioned that the skills required for graduate school success are different from those that brought success as an undergrad. We feel there are two primary differences. First, there is the change in autonomy. Because things aren't often so spelled out, you have to become an active problem solver. You have to determine the best course of action, the resources to utilize, the time to devote, and so on. If you are not actively running towards your goal, you're likely to stay in graduate school longer than you initially intended. Second, there is the change in feasibility. We previously mentioned that as an undergraduate, most (if not all) the tasks you were assigned had solutions. And, they were solvable within the assigned time window. For example, no matter how difficult a problem set looked, you knew that it had been assigned before and that others had completed the assignment within the allocated time. Some of you are certainly saying, hey, I've been assigned crazy problem sets that were not doable within the allocated time. Sure. However, what happened when none of the students in the class were able to complete the assignment? Most likely, if none of the students finished on time, the professor gave the class more time. If even one student finished on time, then it was possible to complete within the allowed time and most likely the other students would finish if given another week. In research, this is often not the case. The most interesting research comes from problems for which there are no obvious solutions. But let's take the rest of this chapter to discuss some specific steps to getting off on the right foot.

Selecting an Advisor and Research Project

When you first arrive at your new school, you will be very excited. Take the first few months to meet the other graduate students, talk with

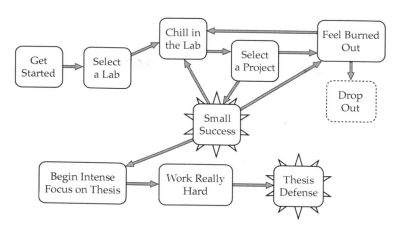

A State Diagram of Graduate School Progress. Students complete a number of smaller projects before they kick into an intense of period of working. There are many opportunities for students to feel burned out; this is natural and doesn't mean you should quit the program.

faculty, and get started with establishing some of the "Tips for Success" listed below. It will take some time for you to discover what works for you. The same organizational tools or software that work for person A don't necessarily work for person B, and that's ok. If you have a goal of making and maintaining at least one non-trivial improvement to the way you work each month, you will be surprised at how efficient you have become by the end of the first year.

We assume that one of your goals for graduate school is to become a world-class scientist. To do this, you'll need to master the skills both of working in a research group and of performing independent research. If you are spoon-fed all your projects then you are significantly less likely to develop these skills. We therefore expect our students to devise their own approaches to research problems. We will help by suggesting directions, tasks, or goals, but ultimately you are the one doing the research. You will have the opportunity to write papers, help with grants, and present at conferences. This may sound daunting, but a good advisor will not leave you stranded. They will provide substantial guidance at the beginning of your studies and as you gain experience, he or she will help you stand more on your own. A good way to think about this is to consider your advisor as an experienced colleague rather than an instructor.

Not all schools are the same, some will assign you an advisor and research group on day one, others will task you with finding an advisor and group. Don't take this task lightly. Selecting an advisor is one of the most important decisions you will make. You will be working with this person just about every day for the next several years. They will help you grow as a researcher, select an appropriate research project, and find your motivation. They will teach you to write research papers and to deliver quality presentations. Think about your personality and determine what type of advisor might work best for you. Do you want to be in a large lab or a small lab? Do you want an advisor that is focused on empire-building or pure academic work? Do you want/need a very hands-on involved advisor or do you prefer less frequent interaction with your advisor? Do you prefer working with someone that is high energy or someone that is a bit more mellow?

The second biggest decision you'll make in graduate school is selecting a research project. Because many projects don't work and all projects face uncertain paths, you are likely to have several research projects through your grad career. This is part of the natural process. In fact, it relates to something we stated in an earlier chapter. The goal of graduate school is not to complete a handful of courses and a research project. **The main goal of graduate school is to learn how to think and how to solve difficult problems.** Interaction with your advisor and the act of contributing to several research projects allows you to gain this most important skill. Consider that in some groups you will be put on a big project and your path to completion will be well spelled out - this may reduce your time to completion but will result in your gaining less research experience (not just time, but dealing with setbacks, coming up with ideas, solutions, working independently, etc).

We typically like to start our graduate students with two projects. One small project that we know can be completed within a few months and a second larger project that could form part of the core thesis work. The smaller project gives the student a feeling of success, it allows us to work on writing a paper in year one, and gives the student multiple presentation opportunities. Once this small project is complete, we replace it with a second, more substantial, project. Most of our students carry 2-3 'major' research projects through the bulk of their time. As we get further along, we tend to focus on the project that is both the most interesting and the most feasible.

People in the Lab

There are a number of different types of people in each research lab.

Each lab is led by a faculty member often referred to as the Principal Investigator or "PI". You are of course familiar with undergraduate and graduate students. There are also postdoctoral students, often referred to as "postdocs". Postdocs are researchers who have completed their Ph.D. and who are receiving additional research experience before going off to an academic or industrial position. Postdocs typically have significant expertise and can be very useful colleagues for graduate students. Also helping out in the lab are lab technicians. Lab techs are more common in experimental labs, they have a high level of applied methodological expertise and help the research group complete experiments efficiently. Computational labs don't typically have lab techs. You may also interact with various support staff and system administrators. These people help with various logistical aspects of running a lab. Support staff can often help with office and financial tasks. System administrators can help you with accessing central computational resources. It goes without saying that you should be polite and friendly to everyone. Treat everyone equally and with respect and they will reciprocate by helping you when you need assistance.

Individual Meetings with Your Advisor

The individual meeting you have with your advisor (typically once or twice a week) is your opportunity to let them know how things are going. You will present what you've worked on since your last meeting and you will propose the next steps. Together with your advisor you will work out any problems that have come up. To prepare for the meeting create a list of topics to discuss. Bring relevant printouts, journal articles, and notes. If you have electronic results be sure to bring them. Bring questions. In addition to discussing research you should let your advisor how things are going, how your courses are going, and if there are any lab issues.

Lab Meetings, Seminars, and Journal Clubs

There are several activities which complement your coursework and research and which should not be neglected. Participation in these activities is an important part of obtaining success in graduate school.

Lab Meetings: Most (but not all) research groups have lab meetings. During these meetings you will discuss lab business, research projects, and newly published papers. Lab meetings are generally the time for short research updates and for tackling challenging problems that you have not been able to solve on your own. While everyone has their own projects, in a successful group, everyone helps each other. Ideally your fellow students' projects are interesting and you should be excited to help, offer insight, and brainstorm. Every PI runs their lab meetings differently. Over time, you'll learn what your typical meeting is like. In many cases, each student will be asked to present a concise (less than 5 minute) research update on recent project happenings. If you've been asked to present your research more fully (you'll certainly know ahead of time) then you should have a longer and more formal presentation. Overall, lab meetings are your opportunity to discuss research as a group. There's a great quote: "be tough on ideas, but gentle on people". It means that as a group you should critically assess and 'beat-up' ideas before pursuing them. If an idea withstands critical assessment then it's likely worth pursuing. It's important to squash bad ideas; don't let bad ideas persist just to be nice to the person who came up with them. At the same time, the group should not belittle or insult team members. Every idea is likely to have some positive attributes. Comment both on what is good and what doesn't work. Be nice to your lab-mates but be honest in your thoughts. This being said, it's very difficult for new students to recognize a bad idea – they simply don't yet have enough experience. So, if you think an idea has flaws, raise these flaws by asking questions. There may be a good explanation.

Seminars: Graduate students and postdocs should be attending research seminars on a regular basis. This means you should attend one or two seminars a week. Every week. Your department likely has one or more seminar mailing lists. Get on these lists. If you are working in an interdisciplinary lab (*e.g.*, computational biology) then be sure to get on the mailing lists of the secondary department. If your department has a primary seminar series you should attend all these talks, even if the subject area is not exactly your subject area. This is another key point. You'll be surprised how often a peripheral idea becomes relevant to your work. In fact, most advances in research come by combining and extending multiple ideas. If you are only attending research seminars in your subject area then you will always be a step behind the field. It's worth rereading the previous sentence.

During each seminar, think about extensions to the work being presented. What could the speaker do next? What could they have done better? What was really cool? Then think if any of their cool results can relate back to projects in your or your colleagues' labs. Not all seminars are good. While you should certainly note and attempt to replicate the methods of an excellent speaker, you should also note and try to avoid the methods of a poor speaker.

Journal Clubs: A journal club is a small group of people that meet on a regular basis to discuss recent important research papers. Perhaps you had an opportunity to participate in a journal club during your undergraduate research. In most cases, there is a leader who selects the papers. Everyone in the group should read the article and come ready to discuss. One person is typically assigned (beforehand) to present. They will often lead the discussion by giving a short presentation. To prepare, the presenter may need to obtain background information from several referenced papers. Most likely you will not be asked to present until you've attended a few meetings. Be observant so that you know what is expected; use journal clubs as a means to improve your presentation and teaching skills.

Keeping a Journal or Research Log

One should never underestimate their ability to forget. To counter this, keep a meticulous notebook (an electronic log is best because you can search it). Unless you can absolutely guarantee that a piece of information is not and will never become important you should write it down. You'd be surprised how many times a seemingly irrelevant piece of information becomes crucial at a later time. Your log should record thoughts, assumptions, experiments tried, details of each run (*e.g.,* methods and parameters), and your interpretation of results. Also record ideas you have and those that result from group meetings and meetings with your advisor. Maintaining a journal is amazingly useful for tracking your progress, preparing for research meetings, and, when the time comes, for writing up your results. We recommend going back and reviewing your notebook once a term. This minimizes the chance that you'll forget to act on an idea or thought. It also allows you to look back on the tremendous amount of work you accomplished that term.

Department Visitors

From time to time your department or research group will host outside researchers. During their visit they will typically present a public seminar, meet with students and faculty, and have lunch with members of the department. If the visitor is in your research area you should try to meet with them (either one-on-one or with a small group of graduate students). If you have a meeting with a visitor, be sure to get familiar with their research before they arrive. This means skimming their website, looking at their active research projects, and quickly reading one or more of their recent papers. Simply being interested in their research is not enough. In your meeting, you shouldn't simply ask "tell me more about your research". You need to actively engage them. When you meet with the visitor you will impress them with your knowledge of their research, you will be able to ask insightful questions, and you will gain a valuable colleague. During your meeting you should also spend a little time describing one of your research projects. This is an opportunity for you to get an expert's insight and advice on your project. If their research area is different from yours, you will gain experience explaining your work to someone who is not in your area. You'd be surprised how many excellent ideas an outsider can provide.

Writing

It takes a long time to learn how to write a good research paper. In a good lab, you will have the opportunity to learn this fine art. When writing your first few papers, you are likely to go through many revisions. Try not to get frustrated with the process or your advisor. It takes a lot of time for them to read and provide round after round of feedback. If your advisor does this, you know they want to help you learn to write. If they simply wanted to minimize their amount of work, they would write the paper themselves. When we work with new graduate students it's not uncommon for us to iterate twenty times on a new paper. Each iteration is completely marked with edits. These comments are solely directed at the writing and are intended to improve the quality of the work – they are not reflections on you. With each iteration, the manuscript converges. When it's complete, you'll have an amazing paper you can be proud of. This can be a frustrating experience for students; however, the ability to write a complete, concise, tight, and crisp paper will go far when you enter the job market.

Over the years we've collected a number of common writing mistakes made by graduate students. If you avoid these you'll impress your advisor:

- Not defining important technical terms, quantities (*i.e.*, 'a large number of results', how many?), processes, etc.

- Assuming the reader knows what the writer knows. Remember the reader doesn't work in the lab.

- Use of colloquial language and phrases.

- Not citing sufficient previous work. Not putting your work in proper context with respect to previous work. Being too aggressive in describing others work.

- Overstating your results. It's good to be somewhat humble.

- Claiming proven results when alternate explanations still exist – only claim something as fact if you've explicitly proven it.

- Hand waving explanations.

- General problems of organization and flow.

Additional Tips for Success

We've touched on the some of the main activities of the first year of graduate school. In addition to the above, we came up with a list of other "Tips for Success" which didn't fit anywhere else. It's useful to review this list (and this entire chapter) every two months through your first year of graduate school. Remember that by incorporating one positive change every few weeks you'll soon be a master.

- Be a resourceful and creative problem solver.

- Continuously ask yourself "How can this be done better?"

- Don't ignore things you don't know. This is a dangerous practice. If you don't know something, first make a solid effort to try to figure it out yourself. If you're still stumped then ask.

- Begin learning your research community.

- Read, read, read. You should sign up for email journal alerts and skim the table of contents of the major journals each month. Read articles that seem interesting. You don't have to work through the painstaking details of every paper, but read to get the general idea. Read the details if you're interested. Read research papers in your subject area (and some outside your area).

- Help others. You are part of a team. Help others and they will help you when you need it. Be an active part of the lab and the department. Learn by interacting with other students, faculty, and visitors.

- Be observant and ask questions.

- Check your work and then check it again.

- Develop an archiving system for important papers, notes, and information.

- Do a thorough literature search at the beginning of a research project and then again at regular intervals. This is the first rule of doing research. You'll be surprised how often you'll find a relevant paper that you never knew about. If you have an idea, chances are someone else has already had the idea and may have published on it.

- Maintain a professional homepage.

- Share both positive and negative results. Nine out of ten things don't work, so it's expected that most of the results are negative results. An experiment is only a waste if you don't learn anything from it.

- If you make a mistake (*e.g.,* coding mistake) let your advisor know as soon as possible so you can fix it. If you've already told your advisor about results generated with the buggy code, let him know that you'll share the new results when it's fixed. Do not hide these mistakes.

- Backup your work.

- Let your advisor know how things are going, both when things are rough and when they are going well.

- Keep in mind what you want to get out of graduate school. Where do you see yourself in 5 years? 10 years? Let your advisor know the answers to these questions.

- Set goals for each semester, each month, and each week. Everything in research takes longer than you initially estimate. We once heard that you should double the number and increase the units by one – so something initially planned for 1 day will take 2 weeks to complete. It's not actually quite that bad. Typically things take 2-5 times as long as a grad student thinks.

- When in doubt, ask!

- Have fun!

We hope this book has provided a useful set of insights into the graduate application process and that you now have a concrete plan for preparing your best possible application. After all, if you're serious about getting a PhD, then you should be serious about making your application as strong as possible. Remember to pay attention to detail and to go the extra mile.

The biggest mistake people make in life is not trying to make a living at doing what they most enjoy. -Malcolm Forbes

Made in the USA
Middletown, DE
25 August 2015